CW00384917

VENICE

A Collection of the Poetry of Place

Edited by
HETTY MEYRIC HUGHES

ELAND • LONDON

This arrangement © Hetty Meyric Hughes
Foreword © John Julius Norwich

ISBN 0 907871 68 2

First published in October 2006 by Eland Publishing Ltd,
61 Exmouth Market, London EC1R 4QL

Pages designed and typeset by Antony Gray
Cover image: The Bridge of Sighs, Venice
by Miles Birket Foster © John Spink Fine Watercolours,
London, UK / The Bridgeman Art Library
Cover designed by Katy Kedward
Printed and bound in Spain by GraphyCems, Navarra

Contents

SIX
Spectral Venice

For Henry Rothstein

Foreword

Venice has always attracted poets, just as she has always attracted painters. Thousands – probably by now millions – have tried to capture her special magic; few – very few – have succeeded. For painters of the past two to three hundred years – the old masters of the *cinquecento* were interested in other things – the challenge has been the ever-shifting light, the reflections of the churches and palaces in the waters of the canals, those wondrous early-morning mists, from which the buildings slowly emerge like materialising ghosts, shimmering in mother-of-pearl. Canaletto could do it occasionally, the Guardis almost all the time; among the more recent, I would award the palm not to Turner but to Monet and Sargent: I have been convinced by no one since.

As for the poets, they have other preoccupations, which are largely those specifically Venetian problems of contrast: of beauty and decay, of happiness and melancholy, of splendour and debauch. The poems included in this most original anthology cover an enormously wide range, but again and again these same themes recur. Venice is by far the most beautiful city in the world, but she is also one of the saddest: never, never would I recommend a Venetian honeymoon.

What is the source of all this sadness? Largely, I suppose, the fact that no city in the world has suffered a more dramatic decline. In the fifteenth century, as the unchallenged mistress of the Mediterranean, Venice had indeed held the gorgeous East in fee; by the eighteenth, she could no longer control the approaches to her own lagoon. She had become the Las Vegas of Europe, a city entirely devoted to the pursuit of pleasure. Her citizens, once the greatest merchants and the most intrepid seamen the world had ever known, were now better known for their prowess as gamblers and intriguers, prostitutes and pimps. In 1797, Napoleon put an end to the thousand-year-old Most Serene Republic, by then too demoralised to lift a finger to defend itself. Batted backwards and forwards like a shuttlecock between France and Austria, mercilessly plundered by the one and bullied by the other, it finally in 1867 became part of a united Italy; but the old independence – and much of the old self-respect – was gone, never to return.

This tragic *dégringolade*, combined with the unearthly beauty that remained, gave the poets a field day. Byron, in *Don Juan* and *Childe Harold*, catches the spirit superbly – though his incurable cynicism often tends to creep in and spoil the effect. But for me, by far the greatest poem about Venice ever written in English – and I suspect in any other language – is by a man who loved Venice more and understood her far better than Byron ever did: Robert Browning. *A Toccata of Galuppi's* is to me, an inveterate Browning-lover, his ultimate masterpiece. Baldassare – or, as he calls him, Baldassaro – Galuppi has always struck me as an unusually boring composer who, incidentally, never wrote a toccata in his life; but who cares? The one poem sums it all up: 'What of soul was left, I wonder, when the kissing had to stop?'

Nowadays, as we all know, Venice is facing a whole new series of perils, of which even Browning had no conception. The constant flooding is bad enough – though this may be alleviated, at least temporarily, by the great barrages which are planned for the three entrances to the lagoon; but what bodes still worse for the city is the steady decrease in its population. Fifty years ago some 125,000 people lived in Venice; today that number has halved, and is still diminishing. There are several reasons: ground-floor flats are no longer habitable; soaring house prices as more and more foreigners (including rich non-Venetian Italians) buy themselves second homes there; and not least the fact that much of the residential building is, to younger Venetians, distinctly substandard – dark, dingy and damp. A young working couple would rather move over to Mestre, hideous as it may be, where they can find large, light, dry and affordable rooms in which to bring up their family in comfort – and run a car into the bargain.

So what is to become of Venice? Every year more of the old provision shops, the *pasticcerie* and *salumerie*, are closing down, the windows that used to be hung with hams and cheeses now crowded with tourist masks of unspeakable kitchness; in another half-century will there be any real Venetian life remaining? Or is the world's loveliest city doomed to become nothing more than a waterlogged museum, the thinking man's Disneyland? Now there will be a new aspect of the city, for the succeeding generations of poets to tackle; and I have no doubt that they will do it proud.

JOHN JULIUS NORWICH

ONE

First glimpses of the celestial city

Venice has always inspired poets, often proving the catalyst for their best writing. Crusaders would stop in Venice on the way to the East while they waited for a ship and write of its churches and impregnable situation. Visitors on the Grand Tour would buy a Canaletto painting as a souvenir and write verses to record their impressions. And Venetians themselves have written lyrically of their magical city.

This volume brings together some of these poems as an introduction to readers and travellers, in the hope of drawing you into the labyrinthine city which inspired them. The selection is directed by pleasure and inclination. This is not a scholarly anthology, nor is it comprehensive. It includes poems which were inspired by the city's beauty, its role as a mighty republic ruling empires and oceans, and by personal responses to the place.

Poems are ordered thematically, to make this a collection that you can dip into easily as you walk through the city or float along its canals. If you're not in Venice but are sitting at home on a rainy day, these poems may act as a fillip to your memory, taking you back there – or as a prelude to a first visit.

By way of introduction, this section is a miscellany of poets' first impressions.

FROM *Sonnets from the Portuguese*
Elizabeth Barrett Browning

The soul's Rialto hath its merchandise;
I barter curl for curl upon that mart,
And from my poet's forehead to my heart
Receive this lock which outweighs argosies, –
As purply back, as erst to Pindar's eyes
The dim purpureal tresses gloomed athwart
The nine white Muse-brows. For this counterpart, …
The bay-crown's shade, Belovèd, I surmise,
Still lingers on thy curl, it is so black!
Thus, with a fillet of smooth-kissing breath,
I tie the shadows safe from gliding back,
And lay the gift where nothing hindereth;
Here on my heart, as on thy brow, to lack
No natural heat till mine grows cold in death.

Elizabeth Barrett (1806–61) travelled to Venice as part of a tour of Italy when she eloped with the poet Robert Browning, who described her *Sonnets from the Portuguese* as 'the finest Sonnets written in any language since Shakespeare'. She was brought up by a repressive father in Wimpole Street in London and was languishing as an invalid: this trip to Italy was an unexpected act of emancipation. She and Browning settled in Florence because the humidity of Venice was detrimental to Browning's health, but she would have preferred to stay in Venice. Her story is narrated by Virginia Woolf in her book *Flush*, the name of Elizabeth Barrett's spaniel.

Arriving in Venice, Elizabeth Barrett wrote:

The Heaven of it is ineffable – Never had I touched the skirts of so celestial a place. The beauty of the architecture, the silver trails of water up between all that gorgeous colour & carving, the enchanting silence, the moonlight, the music, the gondolas ... I mix it all up together & maintain that nothing is like it, nothing equal to it, not a second Venice in the world.

And in a letter from Venice,

Venice is quite exquisite; it wrapt me round with a spell at first sight, and I longed to live and die there – never to go away.

August von Platen

At last I left the open sea behind
To watch Palladio's churches looming near
Out of the water; the waves that roll us here
And hug these steps are guileless now and kind.

We walk off on dry land with grateful mind,
The whole lagoon seems to rush back, and there
Before us the Doge's colonnades appear,
Old, huge, and the bridge that sighs have signed.

Venice's lion, Venice's joy, how high
The kingly brazen wings are towering
From that gigantic stone they glorify!

I disembark with the awe and dread I bring.
St Mark's Square sparkles in the sun. Shall I
Be bold enough to be there, wandering?

August von Platen-Hallermünde (1796–1835) was a Prussian nobleman and fought in the 1814 war of liberation against Napoleon. But he was no natural soldier, so he turned to studying philosophy, classics and through that, poetry. He travelled to Venice in 1824. His journal is said to have inspired Thomas Mann with the theme of *Death in Venice*.

This poem, the first of von Platen's Venetian sonnets, is surely a fair reflection of the excitement and trepidation a first visit can bring, after the long anticipation of seeing such a famed city. He had one more apprehension:

> This labyrinth of bridges and cramped streets
> Which twist and cross and mix a myriad ways,
> How shall I ever master it? This maze,
> How can I penetrate its far retreats?

So he climbed the Campanile in St Mark's Square to get a sense of the topography, in an echo of Goethe's ascent of the very same bell tower, from which he saw the sea for the first time in his life in 1786.

La Madonna dell'Acqua
John Ruskin

Around her shrine no earthly blossoms blow,
No footsteps fret the pathway to and fro;
No sign nor record of departed prayer,
Print of the stone, nor echo of the air;
Worn by the lip, nor wearied by the knee, –
Only a deeper silence of the sea:
For there, in passing, pause the breezes bleak,
And the foam fades, and all the waves are weak.
The pulse-like oars in softer fall succeed,
The black prow falters through the wild seaweed –
Where, twilight-borne, the minute thunders reach,
Of deep-mouthed surf, that bays by Lido's beach,
With intermittent motion traversed far,
And shattered glancing of the western star,
Till the faint storm-bird on the heaving flow
Drops in white circles, silently like snow.
Not here the ponderous gem nor pealing note,
Dim to adorn – insentient to adore –
But purple-dyed, the mists of evening float,
In ceaseless incense from the burning floor
Of ocean, and the gathered gold of heaven
Laces its sapphire vault, and, early given
The white rays of the rushing firmament
Pierce the blue-quivering night through wreath or rent
Of cloud inscrutable and motionless, –
Hectic and wan, and moon-companioned cloud!
Oh! lone Madonna, angel of the deep,
When the night falls, and deadly winds are loud,
Will not thy love be with us while we keep
Our watch upon the waters, and the gaze

Of thy soft eyes, that slumber not, nor sleep?
Deem not then, stranger, that such trust is vain;
Faith walks not on these weary waves alone,
Though weakness dread or apathy disdain
The spot which God has hallowed for His own,
They sin who pass it lightly, ill-divining
The glory of this place of bitter prayer;
And hoping against hope, and self-resigning,
And reach of faith, and wrestling with despair,
And resurrection of the last distress,
Into the sense of Heaven, when earth is bare,
And of God's voice, when man's is comfortless.

John Ruskin (1819–1900) prefaced this poem with the lines:

> In the centre of the lagoon between Venice and the mouth of the Brenta, supported on a few mouldering piles, stands a small shrine dedicated to the Madonna dell' Acqua, which the gondolier never passes without a prayer.

This poem is one of the first pieces Ruskin wrote about the city, after his first visit as a young man in 1835. He was later to write extensively about Venice, and his influence on visitors to the city and writers is almost beyond compare. Jan Morris, herself the author of a superlative book on Venice, wrote of Ruskin's masterpiece, *The Stones of Venice*:

> Ruskin described the buildings of Venice so thoroughly and so fascinatingly that generations of travellers used the work as a sort of handbook, and the Englishman or American following Ruskin column by column along the arcade of the Doge's Palace became a familiar figure of Venetian tourism.

> Ruskin devoted much of his life to researching and rectifying the history of the city's architecture, and to saving many buildings from demolition or insensitive restoration.

Alle Zattere

Arthur Symons

Only to live, only to be
In Venice, is enough for me.
To be a beggar, and to lie
At home beneath the equal sky,
To feel the sun, to drink the night,
Had been enough for my delight;
Happy because the sun allowed
The luxury of being proud
Not to some only; but to all
The right to lie along the wall.
Here my ambition dies; I ask
No more than some half-idle task,
To be done idly, and to fill
Some gaps of leisure when I will.
I care not if the world forget
That it was ever in my debt;
I care not where its prizes fall;
I long for nothing, having all.
The sun each morning, on his way,
Calls for me at the Zattere;
I wake and greet him, I go out,
Meet him, and follow him about;
We spend the day together, he
Goes to bed early; as for me,
I make the moon my mistress, prove
Constant to my inconstant love,
For she is coy with me, will hie
To my arms amorously and fly
Ere I have kissed her; ah! but she
She it is, to eternity,

I adore only; and her smile
Bewilders the enchanted isle
To more celestial magic, glows
At once the crystal and the rose.
The crazy lover of the moon,
I hold her, on the still lagoon,
Sometimes I hold her in my arms;
'Tis her cold silver kiss that warms
My blood to singing, and puts fire
Into the heart of my desire.
And all desire in Venice dies
To such diviner lunacies.
Life dreams itself: the world goes on,
Oblivious, in oblivion;
Life dreams itself, content to keep
Happy immortality, in sleep.

Arthur Symons (1865–1945) was a British poet and critic. He translated the works of French Symbolist poets on whom he wrote an eloquent volume of criticism, and wrote *Cities of Italy* in 1907. He introduced T. S. Eliot to the poetry of Jules Laforgue, and discovered some lost (or bowdlerized) chapters of Casanova's memoirs. He once said, 'Yes, it is difficult to believe in Venice, most of all when one is in Venice.'

Night Litany
Ezra Pound

O Dieu, purifiez nos cœurs!
      Purifiez nos cœurs!

Yea the lines hast thou laid unto me
      in pleasant places,
And the beauty of this thy Venice
      hast thou shown unto me
Until is its loveliness become unto me
      a thing of tears.

O God, what great kindness
      have we done in times past
      and forgotten it,
That thou givest this wonder unto us,
      O God of waters?

O God of the night,
      What great sorrow
Cometh unto us,
      That thou thus repayest us
Before the time of its coming?

O God of silence,
      Purifiez nos cœurs,
Purifiez nos cœurs,
For we have seen
The glory of the shadow of the
      likeness of thine handmaid,

Yea, the glory of the shadow
      of thy Beauty hath walked

Upon the shadow of the waters
In this thy Venice.
     And before the holiness
Of the shadow of thy handmaid
     Have I hidden mine eyes,
          O God of waters.

O God of silence,
     Purifiez nos cœurs,
Purifiez nos cœurs,
O God of waters,
     make clean our hearts within us,
     For I have seen the
Shadow of this thy Venice
Floating upon the waters,
     And thy stars

Have seen this thing, out of their far courses
Have they seen this thing,
O God of waters,
Even as are thy stars
Silent unto us in their far-coursing,
Even so is mine heart
     become silent within me.

Purifiez nos cœurs
O God of silence,
Purifiez nos cœurs
O God of waters.

Venice was one of the first European cities Ezra Pound (1885–1972) saw. He visited Venice at the age of thirteen with his aunt, and it made a lasting impression. He returned several years later and lived in Dorsoduro, opposite the boat yard (*squero*) on Rio San Trovaso. This poem dates from his early days here (1907). A few months later he published his first collection of poems, *A Lume Spento* (1908), at his own expense. But he was nervous, and wrote, 'shd/I chuck the lot into the tide-water?'

Truman Capote, of *Breakfast at Tiffany's* fame, summed up Pound's early life:

Born 1885, an Idaho boy. Taught school; was tossed out for being 'too much the Latin Quarter type.' Soon sought solace amid similar souls abroad. Aged twenty-three, while starving himself fat on a potato diet in Venice, he published *A Lume Spento*, a first book of poems which instigated a fierce friendship with Yeats, who wrote of him: 'A rugged and headstrong nature and he is always hurting people's feelings, but he has I think some genius and great goodwill.'

Pound was imprisoned near Pisa after being arrested by partisans in 1945 for his support of Mussolini and Fascism. Once repatriated he stood trial, and was found unfit on grounds of insanity, which led to eight years in hospital in Washington DC. On his release in 1958, Pound returned to Venice. He died here in 1972, and was buried on the cemetery island of San Michele. He had felt his *Cantos* were a failure. In an interview for a documentary with Pier Paolo Pasolini and the poet Ronsisvalle, Pound said: 'Cocteau called me the rower on the river of the dead: "le rameur sur le fleuve des morts"; it is sad to look back.'

Pomegranate

D. H. Lawrence

Whereas at Venice
Abhorrent, green, slippery city
Whose doges were old, and had ancient eyes,
In the dense foliage of the inner garden
Pomegranates like bright green stone,
And barbed, barbed with a crown.
Oh, crown of spiked green metal
Actually growing!

D. H. Lawrence (1885–1930) was the son of a miner and a
school teacher from Nottingham and is famous for his novel
Lady Chatterley's Lover and the ensuing court case and scandal.
He travelled to Italy with his lover, a German aristocrat who had
left her husband for him, and did not always write whole-
heartedly well of Venice. Perhaps he slithered off the pavement
into a canal in a moment of distraction, or was bitten by too
many of the mosquitoes which used to plague the city. For in his
poem *Mosquito* he wrote:

> I heard a woman call you the Winged Victory
> In sluggish Venice.
>
> You turn your head towards your tail, and smile.

FROM *Venetian Stanzas*

Joseph Brodsky

Golden scales of tall windows bring to the rippled surface
wedges of grand piano, bric-à-brac, oils in frames.
That's what's hidden inside, blinds drawn, by perches
or, gills flapping, by breams.
The retina's sudden encounter with a white ceiling's goddess
shedding it all but her cobweb bra
makes one dizzy. A doorway's inflamed raw throat is
                                        gaping to utter 'Ahhh.'

One of the great Russian poets of the twentieth century, Joseph
Brodsky (1940–96) was exiled in 1964 to northern Russia,
sentenced to five years' hard labour for 'social parasitism'. He
did not serve the full term; still in exile, he settled in the States,
winning the Nobel Prize for Literature in 1987. The lines above
mark his first impressions of the city as he sailed down the
Grand Canal after arriving at the railway station.

Brodsky first knew Venice through the writings of the French
poet and novelist Henri de Régnier.

Sometime in 1966 – I was twenty-six then – a friend lent me
three short novels by a French writer, Henri de Régnier,
translated into Russian by the wonderful Russian poet
Mikhail Kuzmin. The one I call in my mind *Provincial
Entertainments* was set in Venice in winter. Its atmosphere
was twilit and dangerous. For somebody with my birthplace,
the city emerging from these pages was easily recognizable
and felt like Petersburg's extension into a better history, not
to mention latitude.

And so he determined to visit Venice. Here he writes of himself
as an eel escaping the Baltic, perhaps inspired by the poem *The*

28

Eel by Eugenio Montale, whose poetry he mentions elsewhere in his celebrated book on Venice, *Watermark*.

> I vowed to myself that should I ever get out of my empire, should this eel ever escape the Baltic, the first thing I would do would be to come to Venice, rent a room on the ground floor of some palazzo so that the waves raised by passing boats would splash against my window, write a couple of elegies while extinguishing my cigarettes on the damp stony floor, cough and drink, and, when the money got short, instead of boarding a train, buy myself a little Browning and blow my brains out on the spot, unable to die in Venice of natural causes.

Arriving at the Santa Lucia train station, Joseph Brodsky took the vaporetto boat down the Grand Canal.

> The boat's slow progress through the night was like the passage of a coherent thought through the subconscious. On both sides, knee-deep in pitch-black water, stood the enormous carved chests of dark palazzi filled with unfathomable treasures – most likely gold, judging from the low-intensity yellow electric glow emerging now and then from cracks in the shutters. The overall feeling was mythological, cyclopic, to be precise.

His imagination was tickled by what Jan Morris calls the 'fishness' of Venice, writing:

> On the map this city looks like two grilled fish sharing a place, or perhaps like two nearly overlapping lobster claws (Pasternak compared it to a swollen croissant).

Joseph Brodsky died in New York in 1996. He was reburied on the cemetery island of San Michele on 21 June 1997.

Perennial

Jack Clemo

Modern lights in Venice
Do not annul, or even distort,
Tradition's dowry. When the trespassing glow
Saps the haunting moon-flutter on St Mark's,
On quaint shops, canal craft, statues in squares,
The classic soul still breathes uncheapened.

At night-drop in English cities the fagged crowds
Sharpen in illusion, seeing the cold
Steady white wave teem with traffic,
But here no vehicle, no jolt of brakes,
Shakes the ancient road. There are only footsteps,
Footsteps and low voices: you think of lanterns
And torches bobbing a thousand years ago.

Fancy the relevant dream-drawn walkers'
Plod across bridges and islands
To a church rite of a lovers' rendezvous!
Modern light, falling on roads unbruised
By dubious transport, cannot distort,
Much less annul, our primal trysts.

The poet Jack Clemo (1916–94) was born in St Austell, on the edge of the Cornish clay-mining area. He attended the local village school, and thereafter was self-educated, rebelling at the age of thirteen against his religious upbringing. He lived as a poor mystic recluse, isolated all the more by his deafness and experiencing intense emotional and spiritual turmoil. He became an orthodox Calvinist Christian in 1938, emerging from his period of seclusion convinced that he should be a writer and that he had been blessed with a divine vocation for marriage.

In 1955 he became blind, six years after the publication of his autobiography *Confession of a Rebel*. Thirteen years later he married Ruth Grace Peaty, who communicated with him by tracing out words on the palm of his hand, letter by letter.

This poem is from the collection *Approach to Murano*. Clemo wrote of 'Venice, whose glass-producing centre, the island of Murano, became a symbol of the clear-cut, luminous image, contrasting with my bleared and heavy clay idiom.' Visiting Venice for the first time at the age of seventy-one, Clemo felt an affinity with the city during the period of transition as he was leaving his native Cornwall to live in Dorset:

> Canal-veined city: its golden heart now beats
> Congruous to my new destiny.

This visit inspired a sudden, final flowering of verse, with *Approach to Murano* being published only a year before his death.

FROM *Tiepolo's Hound*
Derek Walcott

The backfiring engine of the vaporetto
scumbled the reflections of her palaces,

the wake braided its hair; now I would get to
the roaring feast with its fork-bearded faces.

The emerald sleeve of the immense lagoon
shone on a wriggling wall where she would turn

from the pearl drops on her embroidered gown,
while water lapped the landing with its tongue.

A gondola's crescent shell, the quarter-moon,
slid with its delving prow dividing coin

minted at sunrise, melting the lagoon
with alchemy where sky and water join.

Through some canal's embroidery, I thought,
I'll trace the tread that carries memory

back to the original, where one stroke caught
the bright vermilion of the white hound's thigh.

Behind these lace palazzos was the work
that chance had brought me closer to; aboard

the lace perspective widening in the wake
of the warping ferry, my hope was restored

that, in the mesh of sunlight which was Venice,
whose gulls on pilings mimicked the standards

of the Doge's galleons (providing that empires vanish
while water has one tense and cannot run backwards)

from a small colony with no book for a guide,
I would discover in some flaking church,

with peering pilgrims scuffling inside
water-webbed walls, the creature of my search.

I sat in the small square, trying to control
a sense of swaying on its grid of stone.

Guardi passed, gliding in a gondola.
To walk in Venice seemed a contradiction.

The inspiration behind this long poem, of which these are but a few verses, was a hound painted on a fresco by Veronese ('Dante in paint, but not quite paradise') or Tiepolo – the uncertainty about which one runs through the poem, sending the narrator to Venice in search of this hound. The couplets above describe his arrival.

Derek Walcott was born in St Lucia, in the West Indies, in 1930. He won the Nobel Prize for Literature in 1992. He has an international reputation as a poet and playwright, and founded the Trinidad Theatre Workshop in 1959. His *Collected Poems 1948–1984* appeared in 1986.

TWO

Venice, pearl of the Adriatic

Early travellers were curious to learn about the great republic which had sent Marco Polo and other merchants travelling to distant places and built a city of gold on the wealth of its trade and conquests. Writers recorded the admirable history of independence and resilience almost as much as they described the beauty of this Venus of cities, born from the waves. As Byron wrote, 'Everything about Venice is, or was, extraordinary – her aspect is like a dream, and her history is like a romance.' Mark Twain, visiting the city in 1867, called it 'the oldest and the proudest and the princeliest republic that ever graced the earth'.

Machiavelli described the beginnings of the city:

> Venice was built by numerous peoples who had sought refuge in certain islets at the top of the Adriatic Sea that they might escape the wars which daily arose in Italy after the decline of the Roman empire owing to the arrival of a new lot of barbarians. There, without any particular person or prince to give them a constitution, they began to live as a community under laws which seemed to them appropriate for their maintenance. And in this they were happily successful owing to the long repose the situation afforded them in that the sea at their end had no exit and the people who were ravaging Italy had no ships in which to infest them. This being so, a beginning, however small, sufficed to bring them to their present greatness.

The system which the Venetians developed was peculiar to the republic, but served its purposes well. Venice had 120 doges, from the first in 726 (or even 697, for accounts differ) until the last, Lodovico Manin, who meekly handed the city over to Napoleon in 1797, thereby ending more than a thousand years of independence. Venice later passed into Austrian hands, whereupon Napoleon wreaked as much destruction on the city as he could so as to deprive his successors of its wealth, arts and military strength. A brief interlude of bravery and rebellion saw the restoration of independence on 22 March 1848 when Daniele Manin (no relation to Lodovico) led the city into revolt against the occupying Austrians and proclaimed the Venetian republic to cries of '*Viva la Repubblica! Viva San Marco! Viva la libertà!*' But the Austrians retaliated with violence and finally, after eighteen months' resistance, hunger and deprivation, cholera struck the final blow. The citizens of Venice had to capitulate to the Austrians on 29 August 1849. Manin was exiled to Paris, where he died as a penniless teacher in 1857. Venice remained under foreign control until 1866 and its annexation to Italy, when the citizens of Venice and the Veneto voted 674,426 to 69 in favour of joining Garibaldi's newly formed Kingdom of Italy.

The poems in this section are hymns to the city; between them they trace an outline of the history of this glorious 'umquhile Queen of the Sea', as Ruskin called it.

Before that Exquisite Large Peece, A Survey of the City and Signory of Venice

James Howell

Could any *State* on Earth immortal be,
Venice by her rare Government is she.
Venice, great *Neptunes Minion*, still a *Maid*,
Though by the Warlik't *Potentats* essay'd,
Yet she retains her Virgin-water pure,
Nor any forraign mixtures can endure,
Though, *Syren-like*, on Shore and Sea, her face
Enchants all those whom once she doth embrace.
Nor is there any can her Beauty prize
But he who hath beheld her with his eyes.

These following Leaves display, if well observ'd,
How she so long her *Maiden-head* preserv'd;
How for sound Prudence she still bore the Bell,
Whence may be drawn this high-fetch'd parallel:

Venus and *Venice* are, Great *Queens* in their degree;
Venus is Queen of *Love*, *Venice* of *Policy*.

James Howell (1594–1666) was a Welsh traveller and historian.
He was best known for his *Familiar Letters* of 1621, descriptions
of his travels which became Thackeray's bedside book, along-
side Montaigne's *Essais*. Howell was one of the earliest British
writers to earn his living almost solely from writing.

In his *Familiar Letters* he quotes:

> 'Venice, Venice, none thee unseen can prize,
> Who hath seen too much will thee despise.'

These are the lines which the Spanish playwright Lope de Vega had quoted in his satirical *Gatomaquia* (*The Catfight*), and which Shakespeare adapted in *Love's Labour's Lost*:

> Venezia, Venezia,
> Chi non ti vede, chi non ti prezia.
> (Who understandeth thee not, loves thee not.)

Venice

Henry Wadsworth Longfellow

White swan of cities, slumbering in thy nest
So wonderfully built among the reeds
Of the lagoon, that fences thee and feeds,
As sayeth thy old historian and thy guest!

White water-lily, cradled and caressed
By ocean streams, and from the silt and weeds
Lifting thy golden pistils with their seeds.
Thy sun-illumined spires, thy crown and crest!

White phantom city, whose untrodden streets
Are rivers, and whose pavements are the shifting
Shadows of palaces and strips of sky;

I wait to see thee vanish like the fleets
Seen in mirage, or towers of cloud uplifting
In air their unsubstantial masonry.

The first settlers in the Venetian lagoon built their houses on floating islets of reeds, according to the Roman writer Cassiodorus (AD 523). The Venetians themselves set the date of the foundation of their city as 25 March in the year 421 at noon precisely, and on the island of Torcello. When the island became too densely populated, its inhabitants moved to the islet of Rialto, dismantling and transporting many of the stone palaces they had built on Torcello to Rialto, and using them as the foundation for Venice proper.

Longfellow (1807–82) was the most popular American poet of his generation, famous for *The Song of Hiawatha*. (Ezra Pound was distantly related to him.) He taught at Harvard University, then travelled extensively. He translated Dante's *Divine Comedy* as well as writing six sonnets on him. He wrote this sonnet in 1842. By then he must have forgotten the incident when he was sitting on the Ponte della Paglia, facing the Bridge of Sighs, one cold December day in 1828: 'a wench of a chambermaid emptied a pitcher of water from a window of the palace directly upon my head. I came very near slipping into the canal.'

D. H. Lawrence

There was a lion in Judah
Which whelped, and was Mark.

But winged.
A lion with wings.
At least at Venice.
Even as late as Daniele Manin.

Why should he have wings?
Is he to be a bird also?
Or a spirit?
Or a winged thought?
Or a soaring consciousness?

Evidently he is all that,
The lion of the spirit.

Lawrence wrote these lines, from the collection *Evangelic Beasts*, about the lion commonly associated with Saint Mark and symbol of the Venetian republic. Lions abound in Venice: in Campo Manin a relatively modern, enormous lion crouches at the feet of Venice's revolutionary hero Daniele Manin. Another stands proudly on top of one of the two pillars in the Piazzetta, guarding the Doges' Palace. Saint Mark was not, in fact, Venice's patron saint from the start. It was once Saint Theodore, who is on the other pillar, on his crocodile. Ezra Pound wrote of this crocodile in his *Cantos*:

I came here in my young youth
   and lay there under the crocodile
By the column, looking East on Friday,
And I said: Tomorrow I will lie on the South side
And the day after, south west.
And at night they sang in the gondolas
And in the barche with lanthorns;
The prows rose silver on silver
   taking light in the darkness.

As Venice grew richer and more powerful, it sought a new patron saint of higher stature. The body of Saint Mark was stolen and smuggled back from Alexandria by two Venetian merchants in 828: they wrapped the corpse in pork, calculating that the Muslim customs officers wouldn't trouble to look inside such a parcel. And so Saint Mark supplanted Saint Theodore, and the Evangelist's lion became the famous symbol of Venice throughout its empire.

St Mark's

Vyacheslav Ivanovich Ivanov

Constantinople sunlight is inlaid,
Locked in the porphyries' and agates' dark,
And so you stand, stooped, like a patriarch
In rich and heavy robes of forged brocade,

With candles raised in horn-shaped chandeliers
(Two in your left hand, three are in your right),
While this world's galleys and frigates bring bright
Treasuries with their keys and samples here

Into the pyx of God inside the apse,
Serving the sceptres of aristocratic
Doges crowned by Phrygian skullcaps,

Near emerald waves of the Adriatic;
Byzantium's rose reddens every tone
Where a winged lion with a book is stone.

The cornucopia of ornamentation inside and on the façades of
the Basilica is the product of centuries of looting: when Venetians
left for the Crusades, they were expected to return victorious,
laden with porphyry and marbles with which to pay homage to
their patron saint. The French poet Théophile Gautier called
the Basilica 'a church of pirates'. Fine examples of this pillage
are the two Greek sixth-century carved marble pillars on the
Piazzetta side of the Basilica, and the nearby porphyry statues
of four men, known as the tetrarchs, probably fourth-century
Syrian. The crowning glory of all are the horses above the main
entrance to the Basilica, symbols of the city's free spirit and

supremacy. They were looted from Constantinople after the Fourth Crusade in 1204.

Vyacheslav Ivanovich Ivanov (1866–1949) was a supreme master of the sonnet, a form normally shunned by Russian poets. He was considered to be the very king of the Russian symbolists. He met his wife Lydia in Rome in 1894, and visited Venice with her, and again on his own after her death in 1907. He returned in 1910 with Lydia's daughter from a previous relationship, Viera, whom he later married.

Scene in Venice
FROM *The Ecclesiastical Sonnets*
William Wordsworth

Black Demons hovering o'er his mitred head,
To Caesar's Successor the Pontiff spake;
'Ere I absolve thee, stoop! that on thy neck
Levelled with earth this foot of mine may tread.'
Then he, who to the altar had been led,
He, whose strong arm the Orient could not check,
He, who had held the Soldan at his beck,
Stooped, of all glory disinherited,
And even the common dignity of man! –
Amazement strikes the crowd: while many turn
Their eyes away in sorrow, others burn
With scorn, invoking a vindictive ban
From outraged Nature; but the sense of most
In abject sympathy with power is lost.

The event which inspired this sonnet is the exceptional day on
24 July 1177 when roles and hierarchies were reversed and the
Emperor Frederick Barbarossa asked pardon of Pope Alexander
III, whom he had driven from Rome into exile. The story has it
that the great Emperor removed his cloak, symbol of his office, and
lay full length on the ground in front the Basilica. The Pope
then placed his foot on his neck, saying 'I will tread on the asp
and the basilisk.' The Emperor ventured the remark that he was
submitting not to the Pope but to Saint Peter. 'To both of us,'
said Alexander. The spot is still marked by a slab in the floor in
the entrance to the Basilica. Samuel Rogers wrote of this event:

> In that temple-porch
> (The brass is gone, the porphyry remains,)

Did Barbarossa fling his mantle off,
And, kneeling, on his neck receive the foot
of the proud Pontiff.

The Venetians like to say that when the Pope fled from Rome and sought refuge in Venice, he hid in one of the city's monasteries, working as a cook.

William Wordsworth (1770–1850) wrote his *Ecclesiastical Sonnets* when he was fifty-one, taking upon himself the burden of writing about the history of the Church of England. These sonnets have generally been less well received than the earlier works for which he is loved, such as *The Prelude*. The following lines from one of them are sometimes turned against Wordsworth:

Haughty the Bard: can these meek doctrines blight
His transports? wither his heroic strains?

Byron was rude about him in the same breath as he brought down Southey, another poet contemporary to him. As early as 1814, he wrote 'Southey should have been a parish-clerk, and Wordsworth a man-midwife – both in darkness.' Later, W. H. Auden was to write in his poem of 1936, *Letter to Lord Byron*:

I'm also glad to find I've your authority
    For finding Wordsworth a most bleak old bore,
Though I'm afraid we're in a sad minority
    For every year his followers get more,
    Their number must have doubled since the war.

Dante Alighieri

To yet another bridge we made our way –
    I needn't tell you what we talked about –
    till, on the summit of the carriageway

we paused to peer into another bit
    of hell, and hear the usual lamentations.
    It was hot down there, and black as your boot.

As in the Arsenal of the Venetians
    they boil cauldrons full of pitch as thick
    as shit, for caulking ships of every nation –

leaking hulks in dry dock, others slick
    with new paint, their planks patched and plugged
                  with tow,
    the climate odoriferous and toxic,

workmen hammering at stern and bow,
    or splicing ropes, fixing oars, cutting wire,
    boys with buckets dashing to and fro:

so, here, but heated by God-power, not fire,
    tar glopped and sputtered into the ditch. This,
    the dead black glue of the infernal mire,

I saw, except for all the boil and hiss
    I couldn't see a thing, for nothing came
    of it but bubbles, bursting as they kissed.

These opening lines of Canto XXI of Dante's *Inferno* were inspired by the industriousness of the shipyards of the Arsenale.

For centuries this was the engine room of the city, sending out ships to conquer lands, trade Murano glass, rich fabrics, salt and spices, and wage wars against the Turks. Visitors to Venice would come here to admire galleons being built and launched in a single day, the hull being equipped with ropes, oars, mast, anchor and finally sailors, all handed out from the windows of warehouses into the ship below as it sailed down the central canal of the Arsenale. In the sixteenth-century war against the Turks, a new galley left the boatyard every morning for a hundred days. The bridge now crossing that canal is the Ponte del Paradiso, named after Dante's poem.

Dante Alighieri (1265–1321) visited Venice in 1321, and the plaque to him on the Renaissance gateway at the Arsenale testifies to how much he enjoyed his visit. He was in fact sent to Venice on an ambassadorial mission which was a wash-out, and he reported that the Venetians were ignorant of Latin and Italian and had a shameful system of ruling. He wasn't particularly impressed by their hospitality, either. One story relates that he was invited by the Doge to dinner, and was given smaller fish than the other guests. So he put one of these small fry to his ear. The Doge asked what this was about, and Dante replied that since his father had died in those waters, he was asking the fish for news of him. 'Well, and what is it saying?' asked the Doge. 'It says', replied Dante, 'that it's too small and young to know.' The Doge laughed and had a bigger fish served to him. Dante died in Ravenna soon after his return from Venice.

Dante inspired every generation of poets writing on Venice. Byron rightly claimed that his *Inferno* is the best of the three volumes that make up *The Divine Comedy*:

Dante is more humane in his *Hell* for he places his unfortunate lovers (Francesca of Rimini & Paolo whose case fell a good deal short of *ours* – though sufficiently naughty) in company – and though they suffer – it is at least together.

The *Inferno* has recently been translated afresh by the Belfast poet Ciaran Carson (born 1948), which is the version quoted above. It's racier, more colloquial and more surprising than any other translation into English of the great poem – more Dantesque altogether.

FROM *The Picture of Dorian Gray*
Oscar Wilde

As soon as he was alone, he lit a cigarette and began sketching upon a piece of paper, drawing first flowers and bits of architecture, and then human faces. Suddenly he remarked that every face that he drew seemed to have a fantastic likeness to Basil Hallward. He frowned, and getting up, went over to the bookcase and took out a volume at hazard. He was determined that he would not think about what had happened until it became absolutely necessary that he should do so.

When he had stretched himself on the sofa, he looked at the title-page of the book. It was Gautier's *Émaux et Camées*, Charpentier's Japanese-paper edition, with the Jacquemart etching. The binding was of citron-green leather, with a design of gilt trellis-work and dotted pomegranates. It had been given to him by Adrian Singleton. As he turned over the pages, his eye fell on the poem about the hand of Lacenaire, the cold yellow hand 'du supplice encore mal lavée', with its downy red hairs and its 'doigts de faune'. He glanced at his own white taper fingers, shuddering slightly in spite of himself, and passed on, till he came to those lovely stanzas upon Venice:

> To see, her bosom covered o'er
> With pearls, her body suave,
> The Adriatic Venus soar
> On sound's chromatic wave.
>
> The domes that on the water dwell
> Pursue the melody
> In clear-drawn cadences, and swell
> Like breasts of love that sigh.

My chains around a pillar cast,
I land before a fair
And rosy-pale façade at last,
Upon a marble stair.

Oscar Wilde (1854–1900) wrote in a letter, 'Believe me, Venice in beauty of architecture and colour is beyond description. It is the meeting-place of the Byzantine and Italian art – a city belonging to the *East* as much as to the West.' He went to Venice when he was a student, in the summer vacations of 1875. Truman Capote later wrote:

I was perfectly happy there [in Venice], except of course that it is incredibly noisy: not ordinary city noise, but ceaseless argument of human voices, scudding oars, running feet. It was once suggested that Oscar Wilde retire there from the world. 'And become a monument for tourists?' he asked.

The houses that walk on the waters

Andrea Zanzotto

The houses that walk on the waters
and want to welcome me
if I go down from evening,
the houses that walk on the waters:
you, who accept the canals' gentle clasp
and let yourself be seen
in all your naked grace
until my tears veil you
until my love
transforms you to
the springtime of my words

The great Italian contemporary poet Andrea Zanzotto was born
in Pieve di Soligo in 1921. He was a primary-school teacher in
his native town. He began writing in the 1940s when he was a
member of the Italian Resistance during the Second World War.
He collaborated with Federico Fellini on the film *Casanova*.

THREE

Songs of love: the gondola

Like many visitors before him, the German poet Johann Wolfgang Goethe had heard of the gondoliers' songs, how they would call out to each other across the water, replying to each other in alternate verses of the great Italian epic poets Dante, Torquato Tasso and Ludovico Ariosto. His manservant then told him he should hear the women at Malamocco and Palestrina, fishing villages near the Lido, singing Tasso. Goethe wrote on 7 October 1786:

> It's their custom, when their menfolk are fishing out at sea, to sit on the shore in the evening and sing these songs in their carrying voices until they hear the men singing back from far out, so it's a conversation. Don't you think that's lovely? Very lovely! It's easy to imagine that someone *listening* close by might take no pleasure in these voices as they struggle with the waves of the ocean. But how human and true the idea behind the singing is. How this melody comes alive for me now, where before we so often puzzled over its dead letters. Song of a lone person into the far distance, that another of like mind may hear and answer him.

But this visit did breathe music into Goethe's writing: it inspired his *Venetian Epigrams* of 1790–95 and these lines:

> I say this gondola's just like a cradle, it rocks me so gently,
> And its cabin on top's like a big coffin. Indeed!
> Thus from cradle to grave through our life we are
> rocking and floating
> As on a Grand Canal, carefree betwixt and between.

These verses were subsequently copied by countless writers, and Goethe's epigram was translated and reworked, influencing a generation of romantic writers. Byron was to write, 'Goethe I am told is my professed patron and protector', and many Russian poets wove Goethe's images of the gondola into their own verses of love and death and poignant longing for a city few of them ever visited.

FROM *Jerusalem Delivered*

Torquato Tasso

The whiles some one did chaunt this lovely lay;
  Ah see, who so faire thing doest faine to see,
  In springing flowre the image of thy day;
  Ah see the Virgin Rose, how sweetly shee
  Doth first peepe forth with bashfull modestee,
  That fairer seemes, the lesse ye see her may;
  Lo see soone after, how more bold and free
  Her bared bosome she doth broad display;
Loe see soone after, how she fades, and falles away.

So passeth, in the passing of a day,
  Of mortall life the leafe, the bud, the flowre,
  Ne more doth flourish after first decay,
  That earst was sought to decke both bed and bowre,
  Of many a Ladie, and many a Paramowre:
  Gather therefore the Rose, whilest yet is prime,
  For soone comes age, that will her pride deflowre:
  Gather the Rose of love, whilest yet is time,
Whilest loving thou mayst loved be with equall crime.

Torquato Tasso (1544–95) probably began the first version of his *Jerusalem Delivered* (*Gerusalemme Liberata*) in Venice in the late 1550s. He set his Christian epic poem during the siege of Jerusalem during the First Crusade in 1099 – a reflection of the fear of an Ottoman invasion which was widespread in Italy before the Battle of Lepanto in 1571, in which the Venetians defeated the Turks.

These lines, which gondoliers would sing across the still waters of the side canals, were translated by Edmund Spenser (*c*.1552–99), author of *The Faerie Queen*, where gondolas surface once again:

> Along the shore, as swift as glance of eye,
> A little *gondelay*, bedecked trim
> With boughs and arbours woven cunningly.

La biondina in gondoleta
Anton-Maria Lamberti

The other night I took
my blonde out in the gondola:
her pleasure was such
that she instantly fell asleep.
She slept in my arms
and I woke her from time to time,
but the rocking of the boat
soon lulled her to sleep again.

The moon peeped out
from behind the clouds;
the lagoon lay becalmed,
the wind was drowsy.
Just the suspicion of a breeze
gently played with her hair
and lifted the veils
which shrouded her breast.

As I gazed intently
at my love's features,
her little face so smooth,
that mouth, and that lovely breast;
I felt in my heart
a longing, a desire,
a kind of bliss
which I cannot describe!

But at last I had enough
of her long slumbers
and so I acted cheekily,
nor did I have to repent it;

for, God what wonderful things
I said, what lovely things I did!
Never again was I to be so happy
in all my life!

Anton-Maria Lamberti (1757–1832) wrote songs, sonnets, odes and proverbs in Venetian dialect. *La biondina in gondoleta* was a song written for Marina Quirini Benzon, Byron's lover with whom he had an affair when she was old and obese, 'owing in large measure to her passion for hot polenta. During the winter months, hefty slices of this typically Venetian delicacy would be concealed in her ample bosom, and those sitting next to her in her gondola would be astonished to see wisps of smoke curling up from her cleavage.' (John Julius Norwich, *Paradise of Cities*). The song was immensely popular, and many Venetians can sing its melody to this day.

Robert Browning

He sings.

    I send my heart up to thee, all my heart
      In this my singing.
    For the stars help me, and the sea bears part;
      The very night is clinging
    Closer to Venice' streets to leave one space
      Above me, whence thy face
    May light my joyous heart to thee its dwelling-place.

She speaks.

    Say after me, and try to say
    My very words, as if each word
    Came from you of your own accord,
    In your own voice, in your own way:
    'This woman's heart and soul and brain
    Are mine as much as this gold chain
    She bids me wear, which' (say again)
    'I choose to make by cherishing
    A precious thing, or choose to fling
    Over the boat-side, ring by ring.'
    And yet once more say … no word more!
    Since words are only words. Give o'er!

Robert Browning's poem is a song in dialogue between two Venetian lovers in a gondola. In the second stanza the woman asks her lover, whose song in the opening lines is full of the platitudes of Venetian literature, to sing to her with more feeling, and so suggests a few lines to him. Later in the serenade she replies to him again:

The moth's kiss, first!
Kiss me as if you made believe
You were not sure, this eve,
How my face, your flower, had pursed
Its petals up; so, here and there
You brush it, till I grow aware
Who wants me, and wide open burst.

The bee's kiss, now!
Kiss me as if you entered gay
My heart at some noonday,
A bud that dares not disallow
The claim, so all is rendered up,
And passively its shattered cup
Over your head to sleep I bow.

This poem of 1842 was inspired by Maclise's painting *Serenade*.
Browning combined death and love, one of the oldest and most
felicitous marriages of metaphors (or synonyms, indeed, for in
Elizabethan times 'to die' was to orgasm):

She replies, musing.
Dip your arm o'er the boat-side, elbow-deep,
As I do: thus: were death so unlike sleep,
Caught this way? Death's to fear from flame or steel,
Or poison doubtless; but from water – feel!

Robert Browning (1812–89) had a lifelong romance with
Italy, often staying in Venice. He always wore on his watch-chain
a coin struck by Daniele Manin in 1848 commemorating the

Venetians' overthrow of the Austrians in Venice. He tried to buy a palazzo here, and his bitter disappointment when he failed to do so was mitigated by his son Pen's purchase of the very grand Ca' Rezzonico on the Grand Canal, now home to a fine museum. Pen and his millionaire American wife restored it splendidly, to the great admiration of their guests, including Henry James, Edmund Gosse and Ibsen. Browning died at Ca' Rezzonico on 12 December 1889, and a grand funeral service was organized by the city before his body was taken to be buried in Westminster Abbey. The plaque on the side of the palace bears lines from his poem *De Gustibus*:

> Open my heart and you will see
> Graved inside of it, 'Italy'.

FROM *Eugene Onegin*
Alexander Pushkin

Of golden Italy's nights
the sensuousness I shall enjoy in freedom,
with a youthful Venetian,
now talkative, now mute,
swimming in a mysterious gondola;
with her my lips will find
the tongue of Petrarch and of love.

Here is an account of the life of Alexander Pushkin (1799–1837) by Vladimir Nabokov, author of the novel *Lolita* and whose translation of *Eugene Onegin* is quoted above.

His life was as glamorous as a good grammarian's life ought to be. A maze of tragic events led to his fatal duel with a young ex-Chouan, a blond, fatuous adventurer who was hardly aware that the morose black-bearded husband of the pretty woman he courted dabbled in verse. This Baron d'Anthès having recovered from the slight wound he had received after shooting Pushkin through the liver returned to France, had a glorious time under Napoléon III, was mentioned by Victor Hugo in one of his poetical diatribes and lived to the incredible and unnecessary age of ninety, when an inquisitive Russian traveller once asked the grand old man how he had found it possible to deprive Russia of her greatest poet – '*Mais enfin,*' answered the Baron rather testily, '*moi aussi,* I too am something: *je suis Sénateur!*'

Like many of the Russian poets writing about Venice, Pushkin never went there. (In fact he never travelled outside Russia.) But like him, the eponymous hero of the poem Eugene Onegin dreams of leaving St Petersburg society to find romance, starting with Venice. Eugene Onegin's impressions are based on Pushkin's readings of Byron, the French poet Chénier and many others, and his description was inspired by St Petersburg.

Of Pushkin's writings on Venice, Nabokov remarked, 'It is a pity Pushkin used so much talent, verbal ingenuity, and lyrical intensity to render in Russian a theme that already had been sung to death in England and France.'

The Russian poet Lermontov wrote *On the death of Pushkin*:

> Silent the sounds of wondrous songs;
> > Their latest notes have pealed;
> Narrow and dim his resting-place,
> > The singer's lips are sealed.

In a Gondola
Arthur Hugh Clough

Afloat; we move. Delicious! Ah,
What else is like the gondola?
This level floor of liquid glass
Begins beneath us swift to pass.
It goes as though it went alone
By some impulsion of its own.
(How light it moves, how softly! Ah,
Were all things like the gondola!)
How light it moves, how softly! Ah,
Could life, as does our gondola,
Unvexed with quarrels, aims and cares,
And moral duties and affairs,
Unswaying, noiseless, swift and strong,
For ever thus – thus glide along!
(How light we move, how softly! Ah,
Were life but as the gondola!)
With no more motion than should bear
A freshness to the languid air;
With no more effort than exprest
The need and naturalness of rest,
Which we beneath a grateful shade
Should take on peaceful pillows laid!
(How light we move, how softly! Ah,
Were life but as the gondola!)
In one unbroken passage borne
To closing night from opening morn,
Uplift at whiles slow eyes to mark
Some palace front, some passing bark;
Through windows catch the varying shore,

And hear the soft turns of the oar!
(How light we move, how softly! Ah,
Were life but as the gondola!)
So live, nor need to call to mind
Our slaving brother here behind!

The Liverpool-born poet Arthur Hugh Clough (1819–61) taught at Oxford, and acquired a reputation as a political radical. He resigned his fellowship at Oriel College in 1848 to go to join the revolution in Paris, where he became closely acquainted with Emerson.

Clough visited Venice in 1850, when he began the dramatic poem *Dipsychus*. It's a Faust-like dialogue between a tormented youth and a Mephistophelian spirit who represents the temptations of the world, the flesh, and the devil. Like Byron, Clough responded strongly to the beauty of Venice, but was apprehensive because he felt it to be ephemeral. He never completed the work, which exists only in fragments published posthumously. He married a cousin of Florence Nightingale, and later helped in Nightingale's campaign to reform military hospitals. He died in Florence; his childhood friend the poet Matthew Arnold mourned his death in the elegy *Thyrsis* which, like his *The Scholar-Gipsy*, recalls the Oxfordshire excursions of the two poets.

The gondola sliding
Eugenio Montale

The gondola that glides in a flash
of tar and poppies,
the insinuating song that rises
from the mass of rigging, the high doors
that close above you and the smiles of masks
that flee in swarms –
an evening in a thousand and my night
is deeper still! A dull rope writhing
in the water awakens me
layer by layer and I am one with that fisher
of eels so absorbed on the bank.

Eugenio Montale (1896–1981) was one of the greatest Italian poets of the twentieth century, equalled perhaps only by Giuseppe Ungaretti. He grew up by the sea, on the Cinque Terre coast in Liguria, and it's the sea and its storms that breathe life into his first collection, *Bones of the Cuttlefish* (*Ossi di seppia*).

In 1935 he gave up the post of curator – a comfortable, secure job – at the Gabinetto Vieusseux in Florence rather than allow himself to be numbered among the Fascists. He was awarded the Nobel Prize for Literature in 1975.

Venice

Friedrich Nietzsche

On the bridge I stood,
Mellow was the night,
Music came from far –
Drops of gold outpoured
On the shimmering waves.
Song, gondolas, light,
Floated a-twinkling out into the dusk.

The chords of my soul, moved
By unseen impulse, throbbed
Secretly into a gondola song,
With thrills of bright-hued ecstasy.
Had I a listener there?

This Venetian lyric comes from *Ecce Homo*. Introducing it, Nietzsche wrote:

I have still enough of the Pole left in me to let all other music go, if only I can keep Chopin. For three reasons I would except Wagner's *Siegfried Idyll*, and perhaps also one or two things of Liszt, who excelled all other musicians in the noble tone of his orchestration; and finally everything that has been produced beyond the Alps – *this side* of the Alps. I could not possibly dispense with Rossini, and still less with my Southern soul in music, the work of my Venetian maestro, Pietro Gasti. And when I say beyond the Alps, all I really mean is Venice. If I try to find a new word for music, I can never find any other than Venice. I know not how to draw any distinction between tears and music. I do not know how to think either of joy, or of the south, without a shudder of fear.

The Glaswegian poet Donny O'Rourke (born 1959) wrote a Scottish version of this lyric:

> A while back there
> ah wiz staunin oan thi brig
> in thi broon nicht.
> Far awa sumbdy wiz singin:
> in gowden draps it swalt
> up ower thi glebe.
> Gondolas, lichts, music –
> roarin fu, it pourt oot intil thi gloamin …
>
> Ma saul a guitar invisibly transportit
> trimmlin wi fierce, wild, jiye
> secretly sang like a gondolier
>
> Did oniebiddy hear? .:.

Palazzo Berlendis, where Friedrich Nietzsche (1844–1900) stayed, has a spectacular view over the lagoon. If you walk from the church of Santi Giovanni e Paolo towards the Fondamente Nuove, it's the corner house which gives onto the lagoon and onto the Mendicanti canal. Here he wrote *Aurora*. Living in so idyllic a spot, it's no wonder that he was happy: 'It's the only place on earth I like.'

Memory of a fall evening in the Eaden Garden
Jean Cocteau

(A gesture … a gun shot,
Red blood on white stairs,
People flocking and learning over,
A gondola … a covered body …
A gesture … a gun shot,
Red blood on white stairs …

And that was all! … Some fright,
Some friendly words,
And in the joyful gondolas,
The boredom of being only three now!)

Jean Cocteau (1889–1963) made films such as *La Belle et la Bête* and *Orphée* as well as writing poetry, comparing himself to Rimbaud and Baudelaire. On 25 September 1908 his travelling companion and lover Raymond Laurent committed suicide in Venice – apparently because of Cocteau's involvement with another man, Langhorn Whistler. In this poem, *Souvenir d'un soir d'automne au jardin d'Eaden*, written shortly after the incident, Cocteau tells of strolls in the Giudecca garden owned by Mr and Mrs Eden with three others, taken before the incident and then after. Although Cocteau was no stranger to drama and tragedy, his flip indifference in these lines is doubtless affected – to good effect.

Much later, Cocteau wove this episode of his life into his novel *The Miscreant* (*Le Grand Écart*), published in 1923. In it he described the city: 'By day, Venice is the shattered pieces of an ornate shooting-range on a fairground. By night, she is an amorous Negress lying dead in her bath with her tawdry jewels.' Here is the Eden garden passage:

One night when the journalist was going back with Jacques as far as his hotel, he said: 'I live a vile life in Paris. I am in love with this girl who has no inkling of it. When I go back, I can't possibly continue my old relationships, and on the other hand I know I shall find it very hard to break them off.'

'But ... if Berthe is in love with you?' (this was the dancer's name).

'Oh! She doesn't love me. You ought to know that. In any case, I intend to kill myself in two hours.'

Jacques jokingly reminded him of the classic suicide of Venice and wished him good night.

The journalist committed suicide. The dancer was in love with Jacques. He had not seen it and only came to know of it years later through a third person.

This episode left him disgusted with the nauseating poetry of disease. He still had an intermittent fever caught on a walk in the Eaden Garden which was an unpleasant reminder of his stay.

Venice had disappointed Jacques like a stage-set that is warped with use, because every performer erects it for at least one act of his life.

After two hours of walking and concentrating in the museums, the splendour fell on his shoulders like a dead weight.

Half dead with exhaustion and cramp, he came out, went down the steps, saw the Palazzo Dario bowing to the boxes in front like an old singer, and returned to his hotel. He admired the vigour of the couples who go round Venice with insect-like activity. Those who know her by heart and have dipped their trumpets hundreds of times before into the golden pollen of

St Mark show their new sweethearts round the square. This Ciceronian role rejuvenates them. They only paused to sit down in a shop, where the object of their affections buys glass jewellery, volumes of Wilde and D'Annunzio.

Stimulated by his slight fever, Jacques, like us when we recall it, was filled with mounting distaste for this charming brothel where the rarest spirits slake their thirst.

FOUR

Courtesans, carnival and licentiousness

Venice was once famous for its courtesans, and visitors came to meet the most famous of them, choosing them from a catalogue of courtesans and their talents. According to one count there were 11,164 courtesans in 1509, and 20,000 a century later – one for each street, at least. These courtesans were highly educated women, well-read, accomplished musicians, even poets, for example Gaspara Stampa and Veronica Franco. The term *cortegiana* comes from courtier, and the Venetian courtesans were indeed richly dressed women of independent means who lived comfortably, even luxuriously. They sometimes saved money for a dowry and married well. They were tolerated – even encouraged – by the state and respected by the citizens, as they attracted wealthy visitors and their taxes financed the building of ships for trade and war. Courtesans led a more independent life than most of their peers, patrician women who were locked into unhappy marriages or behind the doors of nunneries.

The courtesans of Venice were the queens of its golden age. Venice's commercial decline heralded their demise. The honoured courtesan gave way to the street harlot, and Venice itself was labelled 'the bordello of Europe' by the French writer Montesquieu in 1728. In his *Dunciad* of the same year, Alexander Pope (1688–1744) sent his prototypical modern fop on a grand tour of the Continent, where, at the climax of a series of sites of cultural decadence, the young tourist visits

Chief her shrine where naked Venus keeps,
And Cupids ride the lion of the deeps;
Where, eased of fleets, the Adriatic main
Wafts the smooth eunuch and enamoured swain.

Pope poured scorn over the city in its decline, deprived of the
fleets that had once sailed around the world conquering cities
and discovering new territories. The city was losing its
monopoly over the trade routes to the East along with some of
its dependencies. Venice fell back on partying, and the rich
merchants, idle now, squandered their fortunes on distractions
and dissipation. It became the centre for dissolute behaviour,
irresponsible gambling and promiscuous adventures. The verve
and energy which had built the city's golden palaces was now
channelled into whirlwinds of partying. The Senate saw that
these distractions were an effective way of keeping citizens from
rebelling, and pronounced that nobody who wore a mask was
inferior to anyone else. And so the carnival lasted six months of
the year; disguised and costumed, everyone was equal and
could behave with impunity. As the Australian writer Robert
Dessaix said, 'Venice knew she was trembling on the brink of
ravishment.' This was the Venice loved by the philandering
Casanova, the adventurer and alchemist Alessandro Cagliostro,
Mozart's gambling librettist Lorenzo da Ponte and the spirited
playwright Goldoni.

Until Byron arrived a century later to revel in this decadent
atmosphere and break the mould of writing about Venice,
visitors all too often tended to paint it as a city of vice,
temptation, sin and sexual looseness, forgetting sometimes that
the early courtesans were intellectual, sometimes patrician,
women. Byron celebrated Venice's beauty and beauties, but after
him poets returned to the theme of carnival as a metaphor for

the city's decline. The Victorians, for example, drew comparisons between Venice in its halcyon days and the thriving commercial city of London in the early nineteenth century, seeing the republic's recent fall as a sobering warning that London too may lose its liberty.

But the carnival has long been a rich vein for poets, and not all wrote of it with caution: many sang its kaleidoscopic colours in vivid verse with unfettered enjoyment.

Lines

Veronica Franco

There'll be no gap between merit and reward
if you'll give me what, though in my opinion
it has great value, costs you not a thing;
　　　your reward from me will be
not only to fly but to soar so high
that your hope will match your desires.
　　　And my beauty, such as it is,
which you never tire of praising,
I'll then employ for your contentment;
　　　sweetly lying at your left side,
I will make you taste the delights of love
when they have been expertly learned;
　　　And doing this, I could give you such pleasure
that you could say you were fully content,
and at once fall more deeply in love.
　　　So sweet and delicious do I become,
when I am in bed with a man
who, I sense, loves and enjoys me,
　　　that the pleasure I bring excels all delight,
so the knot of love, however tight
it seemed before, is tied tighter still.

Veronica Franco (1546–91) was featured in the 1565 catalogue of the 215 most famous courtesans of Venice, with her mother listed as go-between. She was famed for her beauty, and Tintoretto painted her portrait. She was sumptuously rich and sought-after. When Henry III of France visited the city in 1574 to be greeted by vast celebrations and displays of wealth, 'even if he was not to be dazzled by the brilliance of the festivals, he was yet conquered by the fairer brilliance of Veronica Franco, the virtuous courtesan, who sang in faultless verse her own *ars amandi.*' (These are the words of the twentieth-century Venetian poet Diego Valeri.) Doubtless her delivery didn't harm the quality of the verse: she was, so the story says, carried naked on a tray to the future king at a banquet in the Doges' Palace. She herself wrote:

> So that I, well taught in such matters,
> know how to perform so well in bed
> that his art exceeds Apollo's by far,
>
>   and my singing and writing are both forgotten
> by the man who experiences me in this way,
> which Venus reveals to people who serve her.

But her poetry hasn't been forgotten: using the *terza rima* form coined by Dante, she sang of love but also of the plight of women, showing her concern that orphans, unmarried women and prostitutes should be provided for. She herself gave generously and sheltered many young people, and founded a hospice for impoverished or retired prostitutes who wanted to make good so that they could marry and lead a respectable life. The building still stands, at Cannaregio 2585, on Fondamenta del Soccorso.

Franco left Venice to avoid the plague (1575–77), and returned to find many of her possessions had been stolen. She settled in the parish of San Samuele, where the poorest prostitutes had their quarters, and died at forty-five. She was loyal to her city to the end, encouraging poets to write in praise of Venice, above all other subjects or places:

Without running on in poetical fashion,
without using hyperbolic figures of speech,
which are all too clearly obvious lies,

    you might have turned your attention instead
to praising Venice, the one and only
miracle and wonder of nature.

    This high ruler of the sea,
lofty virgin, inviolate and pure,
without equivalent or peer in the world,

    this is what you should have praised,
this gentle land, in which you were born,
and where I, too, thank God, was born.

The Courtesan
Rainer Maria Rilke

The sun of Venice in my hair's preparing
a gold where lustrously shall culminate
all alchemy. My brows, which emulate
her bridges, you can contemplate

over the silent perilousness repairing
of eyes which some communion secretly
unites with her canals, so that the sea
rises and ebbs and changes in them. He

who once has seen me falls to envying
my dog, because, in moments of distraction,
this hand no fieriness incinerates,

scatheless, bejewelled, there recuperates. –
And many a hopeful youth of high extraction
Will not survive my mouth's envenoming.

The courtesans of Venice were famous for their remarkable dress sense. Not only did they wear rich jewels brought on Venetian ships from the East: they were the trend-setters in fashion. They would wear platform shoes so high that they stood a foot or two above the two servants who would have to stand on either side of them to keep them from toppling over. A pair of these shoes survives in the Museo Correr on Piazza San Marco. There you can also see paintings of courtesans' wild hairstyles. The most famous of these is Carpaccio's *Two Venetian Women*, which was believed to be a portrait of two courtesans until only very recently. They wore their hair high, curled into horns springing upwards from the forehead, in contrast to their dresses, which were so low as to leave the back – and front – quite naked. Venetian women, like the subject of the poem above, would sit for hours on the wooden perches (*altane*) and balconies of their palaces to bleach their hair in the sun after bathing it in preparations consisting mainly of urine.

Rainer Maria Rilke (1875–1926) headed straight to Venice on his first trip abroad after completing his studies in Prague and Munich. On his second trip eight years later – by then he'd married a pupil of the sculptor Rodin – he lodged with an Italian family. He fell madly in love with one of the Romanelli family, Mimi, and wrote to her in French between 1907 and 1921. In one letter to her he cries out 'My soul has only one desire, to be in Venice!' It's believed that Mimi was the model for the courtesan of this poem. Rilke became Rodin's secretary in Paris (1905–06) and continued travelling in Europe until the outbreak of war, when he was forced to go back to Germany. In a letter of 1920, he wrote:

> Venice is an act of faith; when I first saw it in 1897 I was the guest of an American. It's different now, and so that a little reality should enter into this insubstantial world I was bitten by a particularly virulent flea and am now more or less localized round the itch!!

The war disrupted his writing, and he published nothing until *Sonnets to Orpheus*, the culmination of his poetical expression.

FROM *Othello*

William Shakespeare

OTHELLO:

Her father loved me; oft invited me;
Still question'd me the story of my life,
From year to year – the battles, sieges, fortunes,
That I have pass'd.
I ran it through, even from my boyish days
To the very moment that he bade me tell it.
Wherein I spake of most disastrous chances,
Of moving accidents by flood and field,
Of hair-breadth scapes i' th' imminent deadly breach,
Of being taken by the insolent foe,
And sold to slavery, and my redemption thence
And with it all my travels' history:
Wherein of antres vast and deserts idle,
Rough quarries, rocks and hills whose heads touch heaven,
It was my hint to speak, such was the process:
And of the Cannibals, that each other eat;
The Anthropophagi, and men whose heads
Do grow beneath their shoulders: this to hear
Would Desdemona seriously incline;
But still the house-affairs would draw her thence,
And ever as she could with haste dispatch
She'ld come again, and with a greedy ear
Devour up my discourse; which I observing,
Took once a pliant hour, and found good means
To draw from her a prayer of earnest heart
That I would all my pilgrimage dilate,
Whereof by parcel she had something heard,
But not intentively: I did consent,

And often did beguile her of her tears
When I did speak of some distressful stroke
That my youth suffer'd. My story being done,
She gave me for my pains a world of sighs;
She swore, i' faith, 'twas strange, 'twas passing strange;
'Twas pitiful, 'twas wondrous pitiful;
She wished she had not heard it, yet she wished
That heaven had made her such a man: she thank'd me,
And bade me, if I had a friend that lov'd her,
I should but teach him how to tell my story,
And that would woo her. Upon this hint I spake:
She loved me for the dangers I had passed,
And I loved her that she did pity them.
This only is the witchcraft I have used.
Here comes the lady; let her witness it.

Othello here relates the tale of how he won the affection and then love of Desdemona through his exotic tales of adventure, strength and determination. He would speak to her in the garden of her palace, by the canal. But he is never reconciled to the city, and when he turns his rage against Desdemona, he expresses it by 'bewhoring' her after his jealousy and suspicion have been stirred. He debases her dignity and noble status, thereby showing his anger against the city which reviled him:

I took you for that cunning whore of Venice
That married with Othello.

Shakespeare (1564–1616) based his play on a Venetian story in a collection entitled the *Ecatomiti*. In the original, Iago advises

Othello to fill a stocking with sand and to strike Desdemona on the back, and to kill her so.

Gondoliers point out to visitors both Desdemona's and Othello's houses. If you stand on the steps of the church of Santa Maria della Salute and look across the Grand Canal, the narrow gothic palace you can see opposite, with attractive balcony parapets sculpted in the shape of wheels and only two windows on its upper floor (but three on the *piano nobile*), is the Palazzo Contarini Fasan. Legend has it that it was the house where Desdemona grew up before marrying Othello. Othello's house is on Campo dei Carmini, near the large Campo Santa Margherita. It has a statue of a man looking out onto the canal; the statue used to be black but has been cleaned to white.

Sadly, Shakespeare never had the chance to say, as Petruccio does in *The Taming of the Shrew*,

> Father, and wife, and gentlemen, adieu.
> I will to Venice. Sunday comes apace.
> We will have rings, and things, and fine array;
> And kiss me, Kate. We will be married o' Sunday.

He dotted his play with references to the city – no fewer than fifty-one by one count – even though he never left England. Both *The Merchant of Venice* ('Now, what news on the Rialto?') and *Othello* have Venetian settings, and the city provided ample drama, strife and ambiguity. Walter Savage Landor wrote, 'Venice is among cities what Shakespeare is among men.'

Johann Wolfgang von Goethe

Venice, if all your canals were girls, and if only
their cunts were
Like your alleyways – what city could vie with you then!

For many male writers, this is precisely what Venice was: a city of
readily available love, where prostitutes bared their breasts at
their windows (hence the Ponte delle Tette, 'bridge of breasts',
that crosses more than one canal). At one time male prostitution
was so rife in Venice that this nudity was tolerated, in the hope of
rekindling men's heterosexual desires. In 1443, the Venetian
authorities were so fearful that their race would stop reproducing
that they passed a law making men dressed as women subject to
a fine. Meanwhile, female prostitutes took to dressing as men to
attract male clients.

Johann Wolfgang von Goethe (1749–1832) was a playwright
(*Faust*), poet and novelist (*The Sorrows of Young Werther*). T. S.
Eliot described the German writer as 'about as representative of
his Age as a man of genius can be'. He spent a fortnight in Venice
in the autumn of 1786, while he was working on his play
Iphigenie. 'I wish to God I could keep my Iphigenie another half-
year, people would be able to sense the southern climate in her
even more.' Incidentally, during his short stay he spent more
time pondering the filthy state of Venice than thinking about the
women who inspired these lines which he composed a few years
later.

Then I went through several quarters of the city to get to the
Square and, as it happened to be Sunday I did some thinking
about how dirty Venice is. The authorities do make some
provision. People sweep the muck into nooks and corners, I

see big boats plying back and forth, and in some places putting in, to transport the sweepings, which people from the surrounding islands use as manure. But it really is inexcusable that the city isn't cleaner, since it's really designed to be clean, all the streets have an even surface, and even in the remote quarters they at least have a raised brick edge, where necessary there's a bit of a camber in the middle, and depressions at the sides to catch the water and carry it away into underground channels. Some further basic measures would make it infinitely easier to turn Venice into the cleanest of cities, as she is the most bizarre. I couldn't refrain from making a plan for it as I went along.

Goethe never put these sanitation plans into practice, but he was not alone in being shocked by the poor standards of living in the city. Venice in its decline was overcrowded and there were few green spaces. (The word *campo* for square means 'field', dating back to the times when these spaces were covered in grass grazed by sheep and cows.) Fresh drinking water was sometimes scarce before it was piped in from the mainland from 1884; the marshes around Venice were malarial, and there was the constant threat of outbreaks of cholera and the plague, which decimated the population on several occasions.

A Toccata of Galuppi's
Robert Browning

Oh Galuppi, Baldassaro, this is very sad to find!
I can hardly misconceive you; it would prove me deaf and blind;
But although I take your meaning, 'tis with such a heavy mind!

Here you come with your old music, and here's all the
                        good it brings.
What, they lived once thus at Venice where the merchants
                        were the kings,
Where Saint Mark's is, where the Doges used to wed
                        the sea with rings?

Ay, because the sea's the street there; and 't is arched
                        by … what you call
… Shylock's bridge with houses on it, where they kept
                        the carnival:
I was never out of England – it's as if I saw it all.

Did young people take their pleasure when the sea was
                        warm in May?
Balls and masks begun at midnight, burning ever to mid-day,
When they made up fresh adventures for the morrow, do you say?

Was a lady such a lady, cheeks so round and lips so red, –
On her neck the small face buoyant, like a bell-flower on its bed,
O'er the breast's superb abundance where a man might base
                        his head?

Well, and it was graceful of them – they'd break talk off and afford
– She, to bite her mask's black velvet – he, to finger on his sword,
While you sat and played Toccatas, stately at the clavichord?

What? Those lesser thirds so plaintive, sixths diminished,
                                        sigh on sigh,
Told them something? Those suspensions, those solutions –
                                        'Must we die?'
Those commiserating sevenths – 'Life might last! we can but try!'

'Were you happy?' – 'Yes.' – 'And are you still as happy?' –
                                        'Yes. And you?'
– 'Then, more kisses!' – 'Did *I* stop them, when a million
                                        seemed so few?'
Hark, the dominant's persistence till it must be answered to!

So, an octave struck the answer. Oh, they praised you, I dare say!
'Brave Galuppi! that was music! good alike at grave and gay!
I can always leave off talking when I hear a master play!'

Then they left you for their pleasure: till in due time, one by one,
Some with lives that came to nothing, some with deeds as
                                        well undone,
Death stepped tacitly and took them where they never see the sun.

But when I sit down to reason, think to take my stand nor swerve,
While I triumph o'er a secret wrung from nature's close reserve,
In you come with your cold music, till I creep thro' every nerve.

Yes, you, like a ghostly cricket, creaking where a house
                                        was burned:
'Dust and ashes, dead and done with, Venice spent what
                                        Venice earned.
The soul, doubtless, is immortal – where a soul can be discerned.

Yours for instance: you know physics, something of geology,
Mathematics are your pastime; souls shall rise in their degree;
Butterflies may dread extinction, – you'll not die, it cannot be!

'As for Venice and her people, merely born to bloom and drop,
Here on earth they bore their fruitage, mirth and folly were
                                                        the crop:
What of soul was left, I wonder, when the kissing had to stop?

'Dust and ashes!' So you creak it, and I want the heart to scold.
Dear dead women, with such hair, too – what's become of
                                                        all the gold
Used to hang and brush their bosoms? I feel chilly and grown old.

The composer Baldassare Galuppi (1706–85) was nicknamed
'Buranello'. There is a statue of him in the main square of his
native Burano.

Robert Browning wrote this poem about the fall of Venice
in 1853. He conjures up a gay, decaying eighteenth-century
Venice, a city of delusory sparkle rushing headlong towards its
destruction. The writing is riper than his earlier paintings of the
city, for example in *Sordello* (1840):

> Venice seems a type
> Of Life – 'twixt blue and blue extends, a stripe,
> As Life, the somewhat, hangs 'twixt nought and nought:
> 'Tis Venice, and 'tis Life – as good you sought

To spare me the Piazza's slippery stone
Or keep me to the unchoked canals alone,
As hinder Life the evil with the good
Which make up Living, rightly understood.

According to the art critic Walter Pater (1839–94),

No English poet before him has ever excelled his utterances on music, none has so much as rivalled his utterances on art … *A Toccata of Galuppi's* is as rare a rendering as can anywhere be found of the impressions and sensations caused by a musical piece.

Carnival
Théophile Gautier

Venice robes her for the ball;
    Decked with spangles bright,
Multi-coloured Carnival
    Teems with laughter light.

Harlequin with negro mask,
    Tights of serpent hue,
Beateth with a note fantasque
    His Cassander true,

Flapping loose his long, white sleeve,
    Like a penguin spread,
Through a subtle semibreve
    Pierrot thrusts his head.

Sleek Bologna's doctor goes
    Maundering on a bass.
Pulcinello finds for nose
    Quaver on his face.

Hurtling Trivellino fine,
    On a trill intent,
Scaramouch to Columbine
    Gives the fan she lent.

Gliding to the tune, I mark
    One veiled figure rise,
While through satin lashes dark
    Luring gleam her eyes.

Tender little edge of lace,
        Heaving with her breath!
"Under is her own dear face!"
        An arpeggio saith.

And beneath the mask I know
        Bloom of rosy lips,
And the patch on chin of snow,
        As she by me trips!

The poem above is from the collection *Enamels and Cameos* (*Émaux et Camées*). It features characters from the Commedia dell'Arte, which had its roots in Venice and nearby Padua. Many of its characters can be seen in paintings in Venice's museums.

Théophile Gautier (1811–72) was a French Romantic poet who worshipped beauty, Art for Art's sake. Running against contemporary fashion and taste, he dredged up words from the sixteenth century in order to enrich the language of French poetry of his time. 'I returned with my basket full, with sheaves and splendours. I put upon the palette of style every hue of dawn and every tint of sunset.' He spent August–November 1850 in Venice, and found it close to impossible to tear himself away from the city, as he rushed around trying to see everything one last time:

Our shattered gondoliers cried out for mercy; we scarcely paused long enough to gulp down an ice cream at the Café Florian. Nobody has ever indulged in a similar visual orgy. We would look at the city fourteen hours a day without letting up.

So, we'll go no more a roving

George Byron

So, we'll go no more a roving
So late into the night,
Though the heart still be as loving,
And the moon be still as bright.

For the sword outwears its sheath,
And the soul wears out the breast,
And the heart must pause to breathe,
And love itself have rest.

Though the night was made for loving,
And the day returns too soon,
Yet we'll go no more a-roving
By the light of the moon.

Lord George Gordon Byron (1788–1824) came to Venice in November 1816. Hounded by bailiffs, recently separated from his wife, and infamous for his rumoured propensities for young men and incestuous relationship with his half-sister Augusta, he dreamed of escaping to Venice, 'the greenest isle of my imagination'.

Despite his reputation, his fame as a poet and his popularity with women, when he first arrived in Venice Byron threw himself into Venice: the language – even learning Armenian on the monastery island of San Lazzaro – and above all the women. He first lodged on the Frezzaria, the shopping street near St Mark's Square which takes its name from the arrow-sellers who used to ply their trade there. It goes almost without saying that he cuckolded his host, the draper Segati:

She is in her twenty-second year. Marianna (that is her name) is in her appearance altogether like an antelope. She has large, black, oriental eyes … She is married – and so am I – which is very much to the purpose – we have found & sworn an eternal attachment – which has already lasted a lunar month.

This poem was inspired by his first Venetian carnival in 1817 and the exhaustion he felt after partying even more than usual – 'though I did not dissipate much upon the whole, yet I find "the sword wearing out the scabbard" though I have just turned the corner of twenty-nine'.

During the later years of the Austrian occupation, the carnival lapsed. The opera house La Fenice shut its doors in 1858 for eight years. The carnival was revived only in 1979.

Venice
Mikhail Kuzmín

Then the monkey spread a rattle
Over the Ridotto scene. A
Devil from Cazotte is moaning
In a crystal sonatina.
Signorina, what's the matter?
Why do your two lips so pucker?
Laugh, my lady, laugh: like ganders
Two proud dominoes are strutting.
Now the perfumed madrigals,
Triolets and sonnets sigh there,
Fall as from a horn of plenty
To Ninetta's feet and lie there …
In three-cornered hat, with cut-out
Lemon blouse, Nina, sweet-scented,
Slyly and affording promise,
Seems a myth someone invented.
Did Tiepolo's brush fashion
With a warm cloud these rich satins …
Gold pineapples on the terrace
That was named for Cleopatra.
And the coffee cools. The slender
Moon dives in the sky: parading
Little boat. My light heart yawning …
Cicadas are serenading.
Gold coins crackle. Transient's laughter …
And the wax-bound candle sputters.
Midnight sheds her sparkling spangles
From her dull shawl – no sound mutters.
No rose … but a small rose: Nina …

Hours strike with tiny hammers …
And the clever Cimarosa
Secretly, lovingly chatters.

A *ridotto* was a public place where gambling was permitted during carnival. Married women would invite their lovers – their *cavalieri serventi* – there after the theatre, or friends would entertain each other with music or gambling. Jacques Cazotte (1719–75) wrote the story of satanic seduction *Le Diable amoureux*. The frescoes of Cleopatra by Tiepolo are in the Palazzo Labia, now the headquarters of the RAI television station, near the railway station. The composer Cimarosa lived in Venice. There is a plaque commemorating him on Campo Sant'Angelo.

Mikhail Kuzmín (1875–1936) was hailed by some as the only twentieth-century heir to Pushkin, and reviled by others because he wrote about homosexual love freely, without criticism. He felt that art doesn't have to be heavy to be important, and borrowed from all poetic schools rather than feeling he had to be bound to any single rhetoric.

FIVE

Romantic decadence

The fall of the republic to Napoleon in 1797 and its subsequent transfer to Austria after the Treaty of Campoformio inspired Wordsworth's famous sonnet *On the Extinction of the Venetian Republic*, one of the first great Romantic poems about the city after its loss of independence, crushed by oppressive occupation. Byron then came to Venice and made it his own, bringing fame and poetry to the city and with him friends such as Shelley and Thomas Moore. Venice was suddenly turned into a source of inspiration, a city in ruins but worthy of romantic elegies. It was sliding into a watery grave of its own making, through failure to put up resistance to occupation, but retained its powerful lure, beauty, even as it was fading. The Italian novelist Giorgio Bassani wrote in 1984,

> Venice was the city of the dead *par excellence* for the writers of the early and late Romanticism, and even more so for the Decadent movement of the second half of the nineteenth century. Venice was a spectre sinking slowly into the very same sea from which it had risen a thousand years earlier. The living who still loiter among its marvellous marbles, drawn closer and closer into the snare of the waters of the lagoon, are not humans, but phantoms and spirits of the dead.

The theme of Venice fallen from its glory later developed into a symbol of decadence. A group of French poets took this to extremes, with Gautier, Régnier, Suarès and others writing of the city as ravaged by predatory occupations, disease and decay. All the while they enjoyed long discussions at Florian's in St Mark's

Square, parties in Ca' Dario and strolls in the Giardini, no doubt comforted by the thought that they'd scare the less aesthetically sensitive tourists away from the city. They collected quaint little ornaments, wore monocles and strutted around the city with extravagant ease. Paul Morand described them in his *Venices*:

> They all rallied to the celebrated war-cry of their master Henri de Régnier: *'Vivre avilit'* ('living debases'), pursuing a Walpolesque, Byronic or Beckfordian dream; they would gather at Florian's, in front of a glass-framed painting, 'beneath the Chinese one' as they used to say; they collected *bibelots*, a word that no longer has any meaning nowadays, lacquer writing cases, engraved mirrors or jasper walking-canes.
>
> The older ones among them dressed in black; only Jean-Louis Vaudoyer dared wear English cloth.
>
> They knew their Venice like the back of their hands.
>
> The English have perhaps never loved Florence, nor the Germans Rome, as much as those Frenchmen loved Venice; if Proust dreamed Venice, they lived and relived her, in her glory as well as in her decadence.

This section dwells longer on the biographies of the poets than the other sections in the book, because their remarkable stories have become inexorably entwined with the poetry of the city itself.

On the Extinction of the Venetian Republic
William Wordsworth

Once did She hold the gorgeous East in fee;
And was the safeguard of the West: the worth
Of Venice did not fall below her birth,
Venice, the eldest Child of Liberty.
She was a Maiden City, bright and free;
No guile seduced, no force could violate;
And when She took unto herself a Mate,
She must espouse the everlasting Sea.
And what if she had seen those glories fade,
Those titles vanish, and that strength decay;
Yet shall some tribute of regret be paid
When her long life hath reached its final day:
Men are we, and must grieve when even the Shade
Of that which once was great is passed away.

William Wordsworth wrote this sonnet in 1802, and thereby contributed to the Romantic image of Venice as a city of fallen grandeur. But he did not visit Venice until 1837, when he had already left his best years as a poet behind, and he felt indifferent to the city.

The Victorian art historian Walter Pater wrote:

In Wordsworth, such power of seeing life, such perception of a soul, in inanimate things, came of an exceptional susceptibility to the impressions of eye and ear, and was, in its essence, a kind of sensuousness … That he awakened 'a sort of thought in sense', is Shelley's just estimate of this element in Wordsworth's poetry.

Samuel Rogers

There is a glorious City in the Sea.
The Sea is in the broad, the narrow streets,
Ebbing and flowing; and the salt sea-weed
Clings to the marble of her palaces.
No track of men, no footsteps to and fro,
Lead to her gates. The path lies o'er the Sea,
Invisible; and from the land we went,
As to a floating City – steering in,
And gliding up her streets as in a dream,
So smoothly, silently – by many a dome,
Mosque-like, and many a stately portico,
The statues ranged along an azure sky;
By many a pile in more than Eastern pride,
Of old the residence of merchant-kings;
The fronts of some, though Time had shattered them,
Still glowing with the richest hues of art,
As though the wealth within them had run o'er.

Samuel Rogers (1763–1855) was an influential poet and literary figure in his time. He was offered the laureateship in 1850 when Wordsworth died, but turned it down in deference to Tennyson. A visit to Italy in 1815 gave him the idea of a poem describing the country – Byron had not yet treated the same theme in his fourth canto of *Childe Harold*. The two poets' works have nothing in common other than their theme, but it was perhaps his awe of Byron which made Rogers timid about his own poem, *Italy*. It was therefore published anonymously in 1822. But the second part was published openly in 1828, and badly received. So Rogers destroyed all unsold copies, revised it, and engaged Turner to illustrate it. The new edition of 1830 was a great success, and *Italy* became a seminal work for visitors to Venice, serving almost as a guidebook-cum-souvenir for visitors and a romantic evocation of Venice and other Italian cities for armchair travellers.

Rogers returned to Italy in 1822 and stayed with Byron and Shelley in Pisa. Byron and he fell out, and Byron, who had once admired Rogers, wrote a bitter lampoon on him. Byron then boasted that he made Rogers sit on a cushion under which he'd hidden these wicked lines against him which mocked his cadaverous appearance more than his verse.

FROM *Childe Harold's Pilgrimage*
George Byron

I stood in Venice, on the Bridge of Sighs;
A palace and a prison on each hand:
I saw from out the wave her structures rise
As from the stroke of the enchanter's wand:
A thousand years their cloudy wings expand
Around me, and a dying Glory smiles
O'er the far times, when many a subject land
Look'd to the winged Lion's marble piles,
Where Venice sate in state, thron'd on her hundred isles!

She looks a sea Cybele, fresh from ocean,
Rising with her tiara of proud towers
At airy distance, with majestic motion,
A ruler of the waters and their powers:
And such she was; – her daughters had their dowers
From spoils of nations, and the exhaustless East
Pour'd in her lap all gems in sparkling showers.
In purple was she rob'd, and of her feast
Monarchs partook, and deem'd their dignity increas'd.

In Venice Tasso's echoes are no more,
And silent rows the songless gondolier;
Her palaces are crumbling to the shore,
And music meets not always now the ear:
Those days are gone – but Beauty still is here.
States fall, arts fade – but Nature doth not die,
Nor yet forget how Venice once was dear,
The pleasant place of all festivity,
The revel of the earth, the masque of Italy!

But unto us she hath a spell beyond
Her name in story, and her long array
Of mighty shadows, whose dim forms despond
Above the dogeless city's vanish'd sway;
Ours is a trophy which will not decay
With the Rialto; Shylock and the Moor,
And Pierre, can not be swept or worn away –
The keystones of the arch! though all were o'er,
For us repeopl'd were the solitary shore.

Despite its loss of independence and rapid decline, Byron felt that Venice still retained some of its former glory, through the elegies of poets. Further on in *Childe Harold* he wrote:

I lov'd her from my boyhood – she to me
Was as a fairy city of the heart,
Rising like water-columns from the sea,
Of joy the sojourn, and of wealth the mart;
And Otway, Radcliffe, Schiller, Shakespeare's art,
Had stamp'd her image in me, and even so,
Although I found her thus, we did not part;
Perchance even dearer in her day of woe,
Than when she was a boast, a marvel, and a show.

I can repeople with the past – and of
The present there is still for eye and thought,
And meditation chasten'd down, enough;
And more, it may be, than I hoped or sought;
And of the happiest moments which were wrought
Within the web of my existence, some

From thee, fair Venice! have their colours caught:
There are some feelings Time cannot benumb,
Nor Torture shake, or mine would now be cold and dumb.

Canto IV of *Childe Harold* is perhaps the most famous poem in English about Venice, and forms a great lament over the fall of the city, even if only in poetic and not political terms. 'Childe Harold will be like the mermaid, my family crest, with the Fourth Canto for a tail,' wrote Byron on 1 June 1818.

After his affair with the landlord's wife was discovered or became tiresome, Byron moved to the luxury of Palazzo Mocenigo on the Grand Canal, flush with the sale of his ancestral home in England. Installed in the palazzo which had housed generations of Mocenigos and gave Venice seven doges, Byron lived with fourteen servants and a menagerie of dogs, birds, 'charming' monkeys, a wolf and a fox. He was already famous for his poetry and infamous for his love life, and had become a living tourist attraction, with visitors wandering uninvited around the palace, surprising him even in his bedroom.

Amid such chaos he nevertheless produced some of his Venetian anthems. He wrote his *Ode on Venice* and began or planned his plays *Marino Faliero* and *The Two Foscaris*. He was inspired to write the fourth canto of *Childe Harold* here and composed *Beppo* and *Don Juan* (a loose reworking of the Renaissance Italian epic *Morgante* by Pulci) in close succession.

FROM *Lines Written among the Euganean Hills*
Percy Bysshe Shelley

Ay, many flowering islands lie
In the waters of wide Agony:
To such a one this morn was led
My bark by soft winds piloted.
'Mid the mountains Euganean
I stood listening to the paean
With which the legion'd rooks did hail
The Sun's uprise majestical;
Gathering round with wings all hoar,
Through the dewy mist they soar
Like grey shades, till th'eastern heaven
Bursts, and then, – as clouds of even,
Flecked with fire and azure, lie
In the unfathomable sky,
So their plumes of purple grain,
Starred with drops of golden rain,
Gleam above the sunlight woods,
As in silent multitudes
On the morning's fitful gale
Through the broken mist they sail,
And the vapours cloven and gleaming
Follow down the dark steep streaming,
Till all is bright, and clear, and still,
Round the solitary hill.

Beneath is spread like a green sea
The waveless plain of Lombardy,
Bounded by the vaporous air,
Islanded by cities fair;

Underneath day's azure eyes
Ocean's nursling, Venice lies,
A peopled labyrinth of walls,
Amphitrite's destined halls,
Which her hoary sire now paves
With his blue and beaming waves.
Lo! the sun upsprings behind,
Broad, red, radiant, half reclined
On the level quivering line
Of the waters crystalline;
And before that chasm of light,
As within a furnace bright,
Column, tower, and dome, and spire,
Shine like obelisks of fire,
Pointing with inconstant motion
From the altar of dark ocean
To the sapphire-tinted skies;
As the flames of sacrifice
From the marble shrines did rise,
As to pierce the dome of gold
Where Apollo spoke of old.

Sun-girt City, thou hast been
Ocean's child, and then his queen;
Now is come a darker day,
And thou soon must be his prey,
If the power that raised thee here
Hallow so thy watery bier.
A less drear ruin then than now,

With thy conquest-branded brow
Stooping to the slave of slaves
From thy throne, among the waves
Wilt thou be, when the sea-mew
Flies, as once before it flew,
O'er thine isles depopulate,
And all is in its ancient state,
Save where many a palace gate
With green sea-flowers overgrown
Like a rock of ocean's own,
Topples o'er the abandoned sea
As the tides change sullenly.
The fisher on his watery way,
Wandering at the close of day,
Will spread his sail and seize his oar
Till he pass the gloomy shore,
Lest thy dead should, from their sleep
Bursting o'er the starlight deep,
Lead a rapid masque of death
O'er the waters of his path.

Percy Bysshe Shelley (1792–1822) was an independent thinker, sent down from Oxford University for his atheistic beliefs. He became famous for his poetry and for his defence of liberty against tyrants. After his first wife's suicide, he married Mary Wollstonecraft Godwin, author of *Frankenstein*. They travelled to Tuscany in 1818 with their young daughter Clara and Mary's stepsister Claire Clairmont. Shelley went on ahead to Venice and stayed at Palazzo Mocenigo with Byron and Allegra, trying to persuade him on Claire's behalf to allow her to be reunited with her daughter. But these efforts were interrupted: on arriving in Venice in September 1818, the Shelleys' daughter Clara died.

They all left Venice a few days later, but then Shelley returned – alone – to spend time with Byron, in Palazzo Mocenigo. During his mourning he immersed himself in writing, producing the wonderful *Lines Written among the Euganean Hills* in October 1818, beginning *Julian and Maddolo* and writing Act I of *Promotheus Unbound*.

To distract Mary Shelley, Byron gave her his *Mazeppa* and *Ode to Venice* to transcribe. This clearly was not good enough. Twenty years later Mary Shelley returned to Venice and looked for Clara's grave, unsuccessfully. She looked back to the period of her mourning and wrote:

> Evening has come, and the moon, so often friendly to me, now at its full, rises over the city. Often, when here before, I looked on this scene, at this hour, or later, for often I expected S's return from Palazzo Mocenigo, till two or three in the morning. I watched the glancing of the oars of the gondolas, and heard the far song, and saw the palaces sleeping in the light of the moon, which veils by its deep shadows all that grieved the eye and heart in the decaying palaces of Venice.

I suspect Shelley was having an affair with Claire all along. Allegra stayed on with Byron. She didn't survive childhood, and was buried in the grounds of her father's old school, Harrow.

Percy Bysshe Shelley

Meanwhile the sun paused ere it should alight,
Over the horizon of the mountains;   Oh,
How beautiful is sunset, when the glow
Of Heaven descends upon a land like thee,
Thou Paradise of exiles, Italy!
Thy mountains, seas, and vineyards, and the towers
Of cities they encircle! – it was ours
To stand on thee, beholding it: and then,
Just where we had dismounted, the Count's men
Were waiting for us with the gondola. –
As those who pause on some delightful way
Though bent on pleasant pilgrimage, we stood
Looking upon the evening, and the flood
Which lay between the city and the shore.
Paved with the image of the sky ... the hoar
And aëry Alps towards the North appeared
Through mist, an heaven-sustaining bulwark reared
Between the East and West; and half the sky
Was roofed with clouds of rich emblazonry
Dark purple at the zenith, which still grew
Down the steep West into a wondrous hue
Brighter than burning gold, even to the rent
Where the swift sun yet paused in his descent
Among the many-folded hills: they were
These famous Euganean hills, which bear,
As seen from Lido thro' the harbour piles,
The likeness of a clump of peakèd isles –
And then – as if the Earth and Sea had been
Dissolved into one lake of fire, were seen
Those mountains towering as from waves of flame

Around the vaporous sun, from which there came
The inmost purple spirit of light, and made
Their very peaks transparent. ''Ere it fade,'
Said my companion, 'I will show you soon
A better station' – so, o'er the lagune
We glided; and from that funereal bark
I leaned, and saw the city, and could mark
How from their many isles, in evening's gleam,
Its temples and its palaces did seem
Like fabrics of enchantment piled to Heaven.

After the death of his daughter Clara, Percy Bysshe Shelley
would ride with Byron on the wild shores of the Lido, where
Clara was buried in an unmarked grave. These excursions with
his friend inspired this poem, which he subtitled *A Conversation*
and modelled on discussions between him and Byron. In this
poem Shelley described himself – Julian – as:

an Englishman of good family, passionately attached to those
philosophical notions which assert the power of man over his
own mind, and the immense improvements of which, by the
extinction of certain moral superstitions, human society may
be yet susceptible. Without concealing the evil in the world
he is forever speculating how good may be made superior. He
is a complete infidel and a scoffer at all things reputed holy;
and Maddalo takes a wicked pleasure in drawing out his
taunts against religion. What Maddalo thinks on these matters
is not exactly known. Julian, in spite of his heterodox
opinions, is conjectured by his friends to possess some good
qualities. How far this is possible the pious reader will
determine. Julian is rather serious.

He wrote of his friend Byron – Maddalo:

> He is a person of the most consummate genius, and capable,
> if he would direct his energies to such an end, of becoming
> the redeemer of his degraded country. But it is his weakness
> to be proud. He derives, from a comparison of his own
> extraordinary mind with the dwarfish intellects that
> surround him, an intense apprehension of the nothingness
> of human life. His passions and his powers are incomparably
> greater than those of other men; and, instead of the latter
> having been employed in curbing the former, they have
> mutually lent each other strength. His ambition preys upon
> itself, for want of objects which it can consider worthy of
> exertion. I say that Maddalo is proud, because I can find no
> other word to express the concentred and impatient feelings
> which consume him; but it is on his own hopes and
> affections only that he seems to trample, for in social life no
> human being can be more gentle, patient and unassuming
> than Maddalo. He is cheerful, frank and witty. His more
> serious conversation is a sort of intoxication; men are held
> by it as by a spell. He has travelled much; and there is an
> inexpressible charm in his relation of his adventures in
> different countries.

Shelley drowned when his boat, the Don Juan (the name of
Byron's great poem), was shipwrecked. His body was burnt on the
beach at Livorno. It was a cruel irony that Byron – who was a strong
swimmer and had saved him at least once before from drowning –
wasn't there that day, and that Shelley had written the words 'if you
can't swim/Beware of Providence' in *Julian and Maddolo*. Byron
wrote to his publisher John Murray on 3 August 1822:

I presume you have heard that Mr Shelley & Capt Williams were lost in their passage from Leghorn to Spezia in their own open boat. You may imagine the state of their families – I never saw such a scene – nor wish to see such another. – You are all brutally mistaken about Shelley who was without exception – the *best* and least selfish man I ever knew. – I never knew one who was not a beast in comparison.

FROM *Ode on Venice*
George Byron

Oh Venice! Venice! when thy marble walls
    Are level with the waters, there shall be
A cry of nations o'er thy sunken halls,
    A loud lament along the sweeping sea
If I, a northern wanderer, weep for thee
What should thy sons do? – anything but weep:
And yet they only murmur in their sleep.
In contrast with their fathers – as the slime,
The dull green ooze of the receding deep
Is with the dashing of the spring-tide foam
That drives the sailor shipless to his home,
Are they to those that were; and thus they creep,
Crouching and crab-like, through their sapping streets.
Oh! Agony – that centuries should reap
No mellower harvest! Thirteen hundred years
Of wealth and glory turn'd to dust and tears;
And every monument the stranger meets,
Church, palace, pillar, as a mourner greets;
And even the Lion all subdued appears,
And the harsh sound of the barbarian drum,
With dull and daily dissonance, repeats
The echo of thy tyrant's voice along
The soft waves, once all musical to song,
That heaved beneath the moonlight with the throng
Of gondolas – and to the busy hum
Of cheerful creatures, whose most sinful deeds
Were but the overbeating of the heart,
And flow of too much happiness, which needs
The aid of age to turn its course apart

From the luxuriant and voluptuous flood
Of sweet sensations, battling with the blood.
But these are better than the gloomy errors,
The weeds of nations in their last decay,
When Vice walks forth with her unsoften'd terrors,
And Mirth is madness, and but smiles to slay;
And Hope is nothing but a false delay,
The sick man's lightning half an hour ere death,
When Faintness, the last mortal birth of Pain,
And apathy of limb, the dull beginning
Of the cold staggering race which Death is winning,
Steals vein by vein and pulse by pulse away;
Yet so relieving the o'er-tortured clay,
To him appears renewal of his breath,
And freedom the mere numbness of his chain;
And then he talks of life, and how again
He feels his spirit soaring – albeit weak,
And of the fresher air, which he would seek:
And as he whispers knows not that he gasps,
That his thin finger feels not what it clasps,
And so the film comes o'er him, and the dizzy
Chamber swims round and round, and shadows busy,
At which he vainly catches, flit and gleam,
Till the last rattle chokes the strangled scream,
And all is ice and blackness, – and the earth
That which it was the moment ere our birth.

Byron wrote this ode in 1819, lamenting the Venetians' inertia in
resisting their Austrian oppressors. Soon after, he was distracted

by his love for a young noblewoman, Teresa Guiccioli. He left Venice to join her in Ravenna, then left Italy altogether to fight – and die – in Greece in its war for independence.

The Victorian art historian John Ruskin was unusual for his generation in his appreciation of Byron. He wrote:

> With the sole exception of Shakespeare, Byron was the greatest poet that ever lived, because he was perhaps the most miserable man. His mind was from its very mightiness capable of experiencing greater agony than lower intellects, and his poetry was wrung out of his spirit by that agony.

FROM *Venetian Sonnets*
August von Platen

I seem to hear a long, undying 'alas'
Sighed from this air that scarcely stirs at all.
It drifts toward me from an empty hall
Once rich with joys and zest none could surpass.

Venice came down, though it thought ages would pass,
And the wheel of life turn back, before its fall.
The harbour's derelict, few boatmen call
Along that Riva where beauty brimmed its glass.

Venezia! How proud you once appeared,
A woman glittering in golden folds,
Painted as Veronese saw you, revered!

Today a poet stands in awe and holds
The Doge's giant balustrades; stands seared
By the true tears no visitor withholds.

August von Platen-Hallermünde extolled the beauty – however
ruined – of the city after its fall, all the more poignant because of
the pride which came before the fall:

What can have happened to that race of kings
Whose daring raised these marble roofs and walls
Now turned to sinking, slowly crumbling things?

The Doges' Palace is still a monument to the republic's greatness.
Although its rooms were stripped by fire and later by years of
plunder then occupation, it may yet be called, as Ruskin said,
'the central building of the world'. It was decorated by the
greatest artists of their generation and is a palace fit for the doges

who wed the seas and conquered distant lands. But close to the rich halls and sumptuous paintings were the prisons where criminals and anyone who dared offend the Senate were imprisoned in squalid conditions, gnawed at by mosquitoes and rats, sweltering under the summer sun and shivering in winter. Casanova famously escaped from his cell, and the Romantic poet and *carbonaro* Silvio Pellico (1789–1854) was jailed under the lead roof in 1821 for defending his fellow-citizens' rights under the oppressive Austrian occupation. He would trade his food for paper when his guards came on their daily visits, writing while almost hallucinating through starvation and excess coffee. He was later led to the scaffold on St Mark's Square, where his death sentence was read out. Then, once the crowd's sighs and exclamations of compassion were subdued, the rest of the document was read out, announcing the commutation of his sentence – to fifteen years' hard labour in Spielberg.

SIX

Spectral Venice

Venice casts its shimmering mirages in many minds and haunts many dreams, reawakening memories, nightmares and fears. By night its dead ends, water entrances and dark alleys can conjure up visions of ghosts and murders. One visitor, Lady Lindsay, wrote in her *Venetian Spell*,

> Each palace is a book, a scroll each wall
> The sculptured poems hold our hearts in thrall.

Hired assassins, poisoned chalices and bloody revenge were once more reality than myth. If you weren't struck down by the plague or cholera or hanged from one of the columns of the Doges' Palace for treason, you might happen upon a *bravo* in the dead of night, a lawless brigand who would steal your watch and money then slash your neck with his stiletto and toss you into the canal.

Reality passed into legend, and the *bravi* of Venice became another romantic mystery. Théophile Gautier wrote:

> Each door which half opens has the air of permitting a lover or a bravo to pass. Each gondola which glides silently by seems to carry a pair of lovers or a corpse with a stiletto in its heart.

This section is a rough mosaic of illusions, visions and disturbed nights, ending with musings about the future of the city, which bring these speculations to a conclusion.

Lines

John Addington Symonds

Come forth; for Night is falling,
　　The moon hangs round and red
On the verge of the violet waters,
　　Fronting the daylight dead.

Come forth; the liquid spaces
　　Of sea and sky are as one,
Where outspread angel flame-wings
　　Brood o'er the buried sun.

Bells call to bells from the islands,
　　And far-off mountains rear
Their shadowy crests in the crystal
　　Of cloudless atmosphere.

A breeze from the sea is wafted;
　　Lamp-litten Venice gleams
With her towers and domes uplifted
　　Like a city seen in dreams.

Her waterways are atremble
　　With melody far and wide,
Borne from the phantom galleys
　　That o'er the darkness glide.

There are stars in the heaven, and starry
　　Are the wandering lights below:
Come forth! for the Night is calling,
　　Sea, city, and sky are aglow!

John Addington Symonds (1840–93) was a British literary critic, art historian and translator. From his student days onwards he devoted his life to the study of Renaissance Italy, and was a frequent visitor to Venice in the 1880s. 'When you are in Venice,' he wrote, 'it is like being in a dream, and when you dream about Venice it is like being awake.'

Symonds marrried in 1864, but within a fortnight of the wedding was confessing to a friend his passion for both the sons of Alfred Tennyson. He was naturally drawn to Venice: unlike Edwardian Britain, the city which Byron had called a 'sea-Sodom' was tolerant, its gondoliers handsome. Symonds was nicknamed 'the Platonic amorist of blue-breeched gondoliers' by the poet Swinburne. He took his gondolier Angelo Fusato to England, and would parade him dressed in his gondolier's costume on social occasions, including a visit to the Tennysons.

Venice
Aleksandr Blok

A cold wind off the lagoon.
The silent coffins of the gondolas.
And I, on this night – young and ill –
Am lying stretched out beside the lion's column.

On the tower, with iron song,
Giants beat out the midnight hour.
Mark has drowned its lacework portals
In the moonlit lagoon.

In the shadow of the palace arcade,
In the moon's faint light,
Stealthily Salome passes by
With my bloody head.

All is asleep – palaces, canals, people,
Only the gliding footstep of the phantom,
Only the head on the black platter
Gazes with anguish into the surrounding gloom.

The Russian Symbolist poet Aleksandr Blok (1880–1921) visited Venice in spring 1909, but already he'd written about it, using the mysticism of the beach of the Lido to describe the shores of the Baltic Sea near St Petersburg. So when he finally saw Venice, he instantly felt at home, writing in a letter to his mother,

> I am living in Venice almost as though it were my own city, and the galleries, the churches, the sea, the canals and nearly all the local customs have become my very own, as though I had been living here a long time.

Blok and his wife were staying on the Lido. In another letter, he wrote, 'Actually, it is quite pleasant here. Best of all are the lions, the gondolas and Bellini.' And:

Our rooms look out on the sea, which can be seen through the flowers in our window. From the Lido we can see the whole northern side ringed with high snow-peaked mountains, some of which we drove through. The water is completely green. All this is well known from books, but still, it is very new – a novelty which is not startling, however, but relaxing and refreshing.

It's a stark contrast to his normal state of pessimism, which soon returned: 'I like nothing other than art, children and death.'

The poem quoted above, the second in a cycle of three about Venice, was partly inspired by a painting of Salome with the head of St John the Baptist at the Uffizi Gallery in Florence. By changing the setting to Venice Blok could use the well established association of gondolas with death in a setting which lent itself well to mystery and gloom. He sent this poem to Vyacheslav Ivanov for review, shortening it by two stanzas to its present form on Ivanov's suggestion.

Lines

Osip Mandelstam

For me the meaning of Venetian life,
Sombre and sterile, is a flood of light.
Here she is – with a cool smile
Looking into the aged, blue glass.

The thin air of skin. Blue capillaries.
White snow. Green brocade.
And everyone is placed on cypress stretchers –
Warm and sleepy, taken out of a cloak.

And candles in the baskets are burning, burning –
As if a dove fluttered into the ark.
On the stages of theatres, in idle discussions –
Man dies.

For there is no escape from love and fear:
Saturn's ring is heavier than platinum!
The block draped with black velvet,
A beautiful face.

Venice, your garments are heavy,
Mirrors in cypress frames.
Your faceted air. Mountains of the aged,
Blue glass melt in the bedroom.

But your fingers hold a rose or a phial –
Farewell, green Adriatic!
Why, then, Maid of Venice, are you silent?
How can one leave this festive death?

Black Hesperus glimmers in the mirror.
Everything passes. Truth is dark.
Man is born. Pearls die,
And Susanna must wait for the old men.

Osip Emilevich Mandelstam (1891–1938) was a leader of the Russian Acmeist movement. He once wrote:

No, not the moon, but the dial of a street clock
Shines for me.

After writing an epigram on Stalin, he was sent to a concentration camp by the communist authorities, and died there. The posthumous publication of his work established his reputation as one of the greatest Russian poets of last century. In this poem of 1920 he uses the decay of Venice as a metaphor for Europe after the First World War.

Over the chessboard of the piazza
the last stars linger on their way.
Castles of light and shimmering thin bishops
surround these spectral monarchies.
The empty game, yesterday's war of angels!

Brilliance of stagnant water whereon gloat
a few small joys, already green,
the rotten apple of desire,
a face nibbled in places by the moon,
the wrinkled minute of an eagerness,
everything life itself has not consumed,
leavings of the orgy of impatience.

The man in his death-struggle opens his eyes.
That splinter of light that through the curtains spies
on the one expiating among the death-rattles
is the look which does not look but looks,
the eye in whom the images form and shine
before they are scattered, and the glassy
precipice, and the grave of diamond:
this is the mirror that devours mirrors.

Olivia, blue-eyed lightly-touching woman,
white hands between the greenness of the cords,
the harp of crystal of the waterfall,
she swims against the current to the shore
of waking: the bed, the heap of clothes,
the hydrographic stains upon the wall,
that nameless body who beside her lies

chewing on prophecies and mutterings
and the abomination of the flat ceiling.
Reality gaping among its trifles
repeating itself in disembowelled horrors.

[...]   Moving in dream,
upon her bed of mire and water, Venice
opens her eyes and remembers: canopies,
and a high soaring that has turned to stone!
Splendour flooded over ...
The bronze horses of San Marco
pass wavering architecture,
go down in their green darkness to the water
and throw themselves in the sea, toward Byzantium.

Volumes of stupor and stone, back and forth
in this hour among the few alive ...
But the light advances in great strides,
shattering yawns and agonies.
Exultance, radiances that tear apart!
Dawn throws its first knife.

The Mexican poet and essayist Octavio Paz (1914–98) entered
the Mexican diplomatic service, then worked in France until
1962. He was encouraged to write by a young Pablo Neruda,
who was working in the Chilean diplomatic service at the time.
In Paris Paz was influenced by Surrealism, collaborating on
projects with André Breton and Benjamin Peret. He fought for
the Republicans in the Spanish Civil War. In 1962 he was
appointed ambassador to India, but resigned in 1968 in protest
against the Mexican government's bloodstained suppression of
the student demonstrations in Tlatelolco during the Olympic
Games in Mexico. He won the Nobel Prize for Literature in
1990.

Elsewhere the spirit is summoned back to life
By bells sifted through floating schools and splices
Of sun-splashed poplar leaves, a reverie
Of light chromatics (Monet and Debussy),
Or the intemperate storms and squalls of traffic,
The coarse, unanswered voice of a fog horn,
Or, best, the shy, experimental aubade
Of the first birds to sense that ashen cold
Grisaille from which the phoenix dawn arises.
Summoned, that is to say, to the world's life
From Piranesian *Carceri* and rat holes
Of it own deep contriving. But here in Venice,
The world's most louche and artificial city,
(In which my tale some time will peter out)
The summons comes from the harsh smashing of glass.
A not unsuitable local industry,
Being the frugal and space-saving work
Of the young men who run the garbage scows.
Wine bottles of a clear sea-water green,
Pale, smoky quarts of *acqua minerale*,
Iodine-tinted liters, the true-blue
Waterman's midnight ink of Bromo Seltzer,
Light-bulbs of packaged fog, fluorescent tubes
Of well-sealed, antiseptic samples of cloud,
Await what is at once their liquidation
And resurrection in the glory holes
Of the Murano furnaces. Meanwhile
Space must be made for all ephemera,
Our cast-off, foulings, whatever has gone soft

With age, or age has hardened to a stone,
Our city sweepings. Venice has no curbs
At which to curb a dog, so underfoot
The ochre pastes and puddings of dogshit
Keep us earthbound in half a dozen ways,
Curbing the spirit's tendency to pride.
The palaces decay. Venice is rich
Chiefly in the deposits of her dogs.
A wealth swept up and gathered with its makers.
Canaries, mutts, love-birds and alley cats
Are sacked away like so many Monte Cristos,
There being neither lawns, meadows nor hillsides
To fertilize or be buried in.
For them the glass is broken in the dark
As a remembrance by the garbage men.
I am their mourner at collection time
With an invented litany of my own.
Wagner died here, Stravinsky's buried here,
They say that Cimarosa's enemies
Poisoned him here. The mind at four AM
Is a poor, blotched, vermiculated thing.
I've seen it spilled like sweetbreads, and I've dreamed
Of Byron writing, 'Many a fine day
I should have blown my brains out but for the thought
Of the pleasure it would give my mother-in-law.'
Thus virtues, it is said, are forced upon us
By our own impudent crimes. I think of him
With his consorts of whores and countesses
Smelling of animal musk, lilac and garlic,

A *ménage* that was in fact a menagerie,
A fox, a wolf, a mastiff, birds and monkeys,
Corbaccios and corvinos, *spintriae*,
The lees of the Venetian underworld,
A plague of iridescent flies. Spilled out.

The notion was once held that glass wrought at Murano was so fine and pure that it would burst into fragments if poison were poured into it. James Howell wrote in the seventeenth century that Venetian glass was so clear that it 'can admit no *poyson* to come near'.

The American poet Anthony Hecht (1923–2004) worked as a literature professor in the States. His first collection, *A Summoning of Stone*, was published in 1965. His collection *The Hard Hours* won the Pulitzer Prize for Poetry in 1968. His style has been described as baroque, opulent, laced, and criticized for being ornate and erudite. But his musicality and mastery of rhythm go well with the abundant whirls and curls of Venetian architecture. He captures the essence of the city:

Lights. I have chosen Venice for its light,
Its lightness, buoyancy, its calm suspension
In time and water, its strange quietness.

Joseph Brodsky went as far as to write 'Anthony Hecht is, without question, the best poet writing in English today.'

Bad Dreams in Venice
Peter Porter

Again I found you in my sleep
And you were sturdily intact,
The counsel you would always keep
Became my dream's accusing tract.

Still I dared not think your force
Might even slightly slack my guilt –
This wasn't judgment but a course
Which self not knowing itself built.

It scarcely mattered where I dreamed,
The dead can choose a rendezvous:
You knew that nothing is redeemed
By blame, yet let me conjure you.

For this was Venice where we'd walked
Full tourist fig, first man and wife
On earth, and where we'd looked and talked
You could unravel your knit life.

And now Venetian vapours clung
To every cold and wounding word –
The spectres which I moved among
Came from the phrases I had stirred.

They could not harm you but they bit
Into whatever had not died.
However we might reason it,
Your fate and mine marched side by side.

And those old harshnesses which you
Muttered to me unrestrained,
Like Venice, loved but hated too,
Were all the closeness which remained.

The Australian poet Peter Porter was born in 1929 and emigrated to Britain in 1951. He argued that poetry, 'however desperate the political reality, will help us cope with life in its normal as well as its extreme states'.

Venice as an image for death – or the death of love – has been irresistible ever since it was first suspected of vanishing. For centuries writers have feared that the city would be flooded, returning to the waves from which it arose as if by magic. Some even believed the opposite, that it would be left high and dry. Few have been optimistic about its survival. Goethe's predictions in 1786 only eleven years before the fall of the republic were probably as wrong as his conviction that the city would remain independent:

> Incidentally Venice has no need to worry, the rate at which the sea-level is slowly dropping gives her thousands of years, and with a little shrewd assistance they will be able to keep the canals filled with water.

Sadly, the streets are all too full of water. Not merely because canals serve as streets, or the sea as pavements ('Streets full of water please advise,' wrote the American satirist Robert Benchley in a telegram), but because high tides regularly gorge the canals and squares of the city, causing irreversible damage.

Lines

Diego Valeri

The canal fills and swells,
overwhelming one by one
the steps of the landing, spreading,
sparkling and even, over
the stone shore, rising and rising.

One day, perhaps, it will end this way,
this legend made of water and of rock.
Swallowed up by mud and soft
sands, she will lie beneath a transparent sheet
of greenish crystal: she who was the glory of the world,
an enchanting mirage
in the restless desert of the sea,
now sweetly dead,
supine in the light
of all the gold and the flaming gems
time dressed her in,
a gleaming basilissa, too beautiful
to last through time,
created to be dead.

One of Venice's greatest poets, Diego Valeri (1887–1976) was born near Padua, then moved to Venice. A plaque and verses mark his house at 2448/B Fondamenta dei Cereri (wax-makers' quay) in Dorsoduro. He was Professor of French literature at Padua and a fine translator of French poetry, but his career was interrupted because of his anti-Fascist activities. After the fall of Mussolini in 1943 he became editor of the Venetian newspaper *Il Gazzettino*, but was then forced to flee to a refugee camp in

Switzerland for the rest of the war to avoid Nazi persecution. In an echo of Baudelaire, Valeri called Venice *città minerale* – mineral city.

If nothing is done to save the city from sinking through flooding, Valeri's nightmarish prophecies will come true in a matter of decades, not millennia. The Russian poet Joseph Brodsky suggested one solution. It's rather radical, but there lies more than a grain of truth in the cause he identifies for Venice's subsidence: human error.

Human fault has appeared to be a likelier culprit when it comes to disaster than any *forza del destino*. I would install some sort of flap gate to stem the sea of humanity, which has swelled in the last two decades by two billion and whose crest is its refuse. I'd freeze the industry and the residence in the twenty-mile zone along the northern shore of the *laguna*, drag and dredge the city's canals and seed them with fish and the right kind of bacteria to keep them clean.

Anthony Burgess wrote in 1988:

Venice is the best exemplar of human wit and ingenuity. Despair of man and go to Venice: you will cease to despair. If human beings can build a city like this, their souls deserve to be saved.

The city itself also deserves to be saved for posterity.

Partenza di Venezia
Ezra Pound

Ne'er felt I parting from a woman loved
As feel I now my going forth from thee,
Yea, all thy waters cry out 'Stay with me!'
And laugh reflected flames up luringly.

For now, stay on, at least as long as you can. As Henry James wrote, 'When you have called for the bill to go, pay it and remain, and you will find on the morrow that you are deeply attached to Venice.'

Acknowledgements

Every effort has been made to trace the holders of copyright and to acknowledge the permission of author and publisher where necessary. If I have failed to trace the copyright owner or made any wrong attributions, these corrections will be made in future editions.

I would particularly like to thank all the poets and copyright holders who wrote back to me and were so kind and swift in granting permission to reprint their verses.

If any poet, translator or reader feels that I have overlooked a favourite verse, Eland Publishing would like to hear from them and consider it for inclusion in the next edition.

Venetian Sonnets *by August von Platen, translated by Edwin Morgan, in* Anthology of German Poetry from Hoderlin to Rilke in English Translation, *edited by Angel Flores (New York: Anchor Books, 1960). Reprinted by permission of Carcanet Press Limited.*

Alle Zattere *by Arthur Symons, reprinted by permission of Brian Read.*

Night Litany *by Ezra Pound, from* Collected Shorter Poems. *Reprinted by permission of Faber and Faber Ltd.*

Venetian Stanzas *by Joseph Brodsky, from* To Urania: Selected Poems 1965–85, *translated by Jane Ann Miller and the author (London: Penguin, 1988). The prose passages by Brodsky are from* Watermark *(Harmondsworth: Penguin, 1997; first published 1992).*

Perennial *by Jack Clemo, from* Approach to Murano *(Newcastle upon Tyne: Bloodaxe 1993).*

Tiepolo's Hound by Derek Walcott (London: Faber and Faber Ltd, 2000). Reprinted by permission of Faber and Faber Ltd.

Lines by Ezra Pound, from Cantos. Reprinted by permission of Faber and Faber Ltd.

St Mark's by Vyacheslav Ivanovich Ivanov, from Modern Russian Poetry, edited and translated by Markov and Sparks (Macgibbon & Kee, 1966).

Letter to Lord Byron by W. H. Auden, from Collected Poems, edited by Edward Mendelson (London: Faber and Faber, 1991; copyright 1936 by W. H. Auden). Reprinted by permission of Curtis Brown, Ltd.

Inferno by Dante Alighieri, translated by Ciaran Carson (London: Granta, 2002). Reprinted by permission of Granta Books.

The houses that walk on the waters by Andrea Zanzotto, from Selected Poetry of Andrea Zanzotto, edited and translated by Ruth Feldman and Brian Swan (Princeton University Press, 1975; copyright 1975 Princeton University Press, 2003 renewed PUP). Reprinted by permission of Princeton University Press.

Venetian Epigrams by Johann Wolfgang von Goethe, from Erotic Poems translated by David Luke (Oxford University Press, 1988). Reprinted by permission of David Luke and Johnson & Alcock Ltd.

La biondina in gondoleta by Anton-Maria Lamberti, translated by Laura Sarti. Available online at www.recmusic.org

Eugene Onegin by Alexander Pushkin, translated from the Russian by Vladimir Nabokov (Princeton University Press, 1981; copyright 1964 Bollingen, 1975 revised edition PUP, 1992 renewed, 2003 renewed PUP). Reprinted by permission of Princeton University Press.

The gondola sliding by Eugenio Montale, translated by Andrew Fitzsimons, from Modern Poetry in Translation (no 18, 2001), also *available from this website: www.poetrymagazines.org.uk. Reprinted by permission of Helen Constantine at Modern Poetry in Translation.*

Venice by Friedrich Nietzsche, from Ecce Homo, *edited by Oscar Levy, translated by Anthony M. Ludovici (London: Foulis, 1911).*

Lines by Donny O'Rourke, from Painted, Spoken *(no 2, 2001), also available from www.poetrymagazines.org.uk. Reprinted by permission of Donny O'Rourke and Richard Price at Painted, Spoken.*

Memory of a fall evening in the Eaden Garden by Jean Cocteau, quoted in Cocteau *by Glenn Moulaison, in* Dictionary of Literary Biography, *vol. 258 (University of Ottawa, 2002). Prose quotations from* Cocteau's World: An Anthology of Writings by Jean Cocteau, *edited by Margaret Crosland (London: Peter Owen, 1972). Copyright Éditions Gallimard, Paris, 1999.*

Lines by Veronica Franco, from Veronica Franco: Poems and Selected Letters, *edited and translated by Ann Rosalind Jones and Margaret F. Rosenthal (University of Chicago Press, 1998; copyright University of Chicago 1998). Reprinted by permission of the University of Chicago Press.*

The Courtesan by Rainer Maria Rilke, from Rilke: Selected Poems, *translated by J. B. Leishman (Harmondsworth: Penguin, 1964).*

Goethe prose quotations from Johann Wolfgang Goethe, The Flight to Italy, *edited and translated by T. J. Reed (Oxford: Oxford University Press, 1999). Reprinted by permission of Professor Reed.*

Carnival by Théophile Gautier, from Enamels and Cameos, *translated by Agnes Lee, in* The Complete Works of Théophile Gautier, *vol. XII, edited by S. C. De Sumichrast (London: The Athenæum Press, no date).*

Venice by Mikhail Kuzmín, from Modern Russian Poetry, *edited and translated by Markov and Sparks (Macgibbon & Kee, 1966).*

Index of Authors

Index of First Lines

There'll be no gap between merit and reward 74
To see, her bosom covered o'er 49
To yet another bridge we made our way – 46

Venice, if all your canals were girls, and if only their cunts were 82
Venice robes her for the ball 88

Whereas at Venice 27
White swan of cities, slumbering in thy nest 38
Without running on in poetical fashion 76

Index of Poem Titles

This pocket book of poetry is part of a growing Poetry of Place series, published by Eland. Other titles in the series:

> London
> Desert Air
> Ruins

Forthcoming titles:

> Paris
> Andalucia
> Istanbul
> The Highlands

If you would like to receive our detailed catalogue, please contact us at:

> Eland Publishing Ltd
> 61 Exmouth Market, London EC1R 4QL
> Tel: 020 7833 0762   Fax: 020 7833 4434
> E-mail: info@travelbooks.co.uk
> www.travelbooks.co.uk